Number 120
Winter 2008

New Dir

MW00698402

Sandra Mathison
Editor-in-Chief

Program Evaluation in a Complex Organizational System: Lessons From Cooperative Extension

Marc T. Braverman
Molly Engle
Mary E. Arnold
Roger A. Rennekamp
Editors

PROGRAM EVALUATION IN A COMPLEX ORGANIZATIONAL SYSTEM: LESSONS
FROM COOPERATIVE EXTENSION
Marc T. Braverman, Molly Engle, Mary E. Arnold,
Roger A. Rennekamp (eds.)
New Directions for Evaluation, no. 120
Sandra Mathison, Editor-in-Chief

Microfilm copies of issues and articles are available in 16mm and 35mm,
as well as microfiche in 105mm, through University Microfilms Inc., 300
North Zeeb Road, Ann Arbor, Michigan 48106-1346.

New Directions for Evaluation is indexed in Cambridge Scientific Abstracts
(CSA/CIG), Contents Pages in Education (T & F), Educational Research
Abstracts Online (T & F), ERIC Database (Education Resources
Information Center), Higher Education Abstracts (Claremont Graduate
University), Social Services Abstracts (CSA/CIG), Sociological Abstracts
(CSA/CIG), and Worldwide Political Sciences Abstracts (CSA/CIG).

NEW DIRECTIONS FOR EVALUATION (ISSN 1097-6736, electronic ISSN
1534-875X) is part of The Jossey-Bass Education Series and is published
quarterly by Wiley Subscription Services, Inc., A Wiley Company, at
Jossey-Bass, 989 Market Street, San Francisco, California 94103-1741.

SUBSCRIPTIONS cost $85 for U.S./Canada/Mexico; $109 international.
For institutions, agencies, and libraries, $235 U.S.; $275 Canada/Mexico;
$309 international. Prices subject to change.

EDITORIAL CORRESPONDENCE should be addressed to the Editor-in-Chief,
Sandra Mathison, University of British Columbia, 2125 Main Mall,
Vancouver, BC V6T 1Z4, Canada.

www.josseybass.com

Editorial Policy and Procedures

New Directions for Evaluation, a quarterly sourcebook, is an official publication of the American Evaluation Association. The journal publishes empirical, methodological, and theoretical works on all aspects of evaluation. A reflective approach to evaluation is an essential strand to be woven through every issue. The editors encourage issues that have one of three foci: (1) craft issues that present approaches, methods, or techniques that can be applied in evaluation practice, such as the use of templates, case studies, or survey research; (2) professional issues that present topics of import for the field of evaluation, such as utilization of evaluation or locus of evaluation capacity; (3) societal issues that draw out the implications of intellectual, social, or cultural developments for the field of evaluation, such as the women's movement, communitarianism, or multiculturalism. A wide range of substantive domains is appropriate for *New Directions for Evaluation;* however, the domains must be of interest to a large audience within the field of evaluation. We encourage a diversity of perspectives and experiences within each issue, as well as creative bridges between evaluation and other sectors of our collective lives.

The editors do not consider or publish unsolicited single manuscripts. Each issue of the journal is devoted to a single topic, with contributions solicited, organized, reviewed, and edited by a guest editor. Issues may take any of several forms, such as a series of related chapters, a debate, or a long article followed by brief critical commentaries. In all cases, the proposals must follow a specific format, which can be obtained from the editor-in-chief. These proposals are sent to members of the editorial board and to relevant substantive experts for peer review. The process may result in acceptance, a recommendation to revise and resubmit, or rejection. However, the editors are committed to working constructively with potential guest editors to help them develop acceptable proposals.

Sandra Mathison, Editor-in-Chief
University of British Columbia
2125 Main Mall
Vancouver, BC V6T 1Z4
CANADA
e-mail: nde@eval.org

CONTENTS

EDITORS' NOTES

This issue of *New Directions for Evaluation* addresses the roles and uses of evaluation in complex organizations, offering evaluators opportunities to explore issues that are central to effective evaluation practice. The contributors use the national Cooperative Extension System as a recurring case study that links the issues together, establishing a laboratory that allows a new perspective on these topics for evaluators who work with community-based programs.

Cooperative Extension is a system of institutions that includes every state's land-grant universities, the U.S. Department of Agriculture, and local county governments. The Extension system's linkages across distinct institutions, professional communities, and funding sources create a highly complex programming environment that presents numerous challenges to the practice of successful and influential evaluation. Extension evaluators must contend with multiple funding streams, differences in information needs and timelines, divergent organizational goals and cultures, and diversity in program content and delivery.

The current literature on evaluation practice within organizations contains numerous themes that can be informed by the Extension experience. One, for example, is the use of evaluation to promote organizational learning (Russ-Eft & Preskill, 2001; Torres & Preskill, 2001) while also addressing responsibilities for organizational accountability (Taut, 2007). As a publicly funded entity, Extension must ensure accountability, but Extension evaluators have also sought to use evaluation to promote learning, improve programs, and contribute to our collective knowledge base about designing and delivering community programs.

A second theme is the role of organizations in implementing community initiatives. The development of successful initiatives often faces challenges in areas such as achieving stakeholder consensus, assessing effectiveness, and planning for sustainability (e.g., Scheirer, 2005). Cooperative Extension has a longstanding commitment to strengthening communities through interorganizational collaboration, and the great majority of Extension programs involve partnerships with local agencies, schools, nonprofits, or other organizations.

Yet another theme is the mainstreaming of evaluation within organizations (Sanders, 2002). As the organizational culture of Extension has evolved, evaluation is in the process of becoming accepted as a core value by staff and faculty within the system. Extension has its own online journal (*Journal of Extension,* http://www.joe.org), which gives frequent attention to

evaluation topics, and its own Topical Interest Group within the American Evaluation Association (the Extension Education Evaluation TIG). Extension has also been a leader in developing evaluation capacity within community organizations, using strategies such as collaborative evaluation practice, national workshops, and Web-based instruction. Discerning how evaluation is being mainstreamed within this multifaceted system will yield insights that can apply to many other organizational settings.

Organization of This Issue

The first two chapters set the stage for the subsequent discussions. In Chapter 1, Nancy K. Franz and Lisa Townson present an overview of the Extension system and describe Extension's organizational structure, its programming emphases, and the variety of partnerships that characterize its programs. They also describe several distinct approaches for conceptualizing and delivering Extension programs.

In Chapter 2, Roger A. Rennekamp and Molly Engle examine how evaluation has evolved in Extension over the past century. They describe the gradual changes in organizational relationships and political pressures that Extension has faced—developments that have, in turn, changed the demand for certain kinds of information. They also describe how Extension has responded as an organization, as reflected in historical periods during which particular evaluation approaches have been dominant.

Chapters 3 through 6 address specific topics that are relevant for understanding how complex organizations approach and use evaluation, as well as the challenges that are faced by evaluators in these settings. Extension is woven into the discussions as an illustration of the topics in action. In Chapter 3, Nicelma J. King and Leslie J. Cooksy focus on the requirement to be responsive to different organizational levels within a system—in Extension's case, the federal, state, and local levels of government. The chapter describes how these levels place distinct pressures on the evaluation process and how evaluators can respond. The multilevel setting, though challenging, can also offer creative opportunities for addressing stakeholders' needs.

In complex organizations, the question of locating the responsibility and expertise for evaluation can become intricate. Should evaluation be part of the organization's central administration, or should it be closer to programs that serve the organization's clientele? Michael T. Lambur, in Chapter 4, describes several alternatives existing in state Extension organizations. Drawing on interviews with Extension evaluators, he describes the relative advantages for each of these structures and how they have influenced the delivery of programs.

In Chapter 5, Ellen Taylor-Powell and Heather H. Boyd discuss the promotion of evaluation capacity building (ECB) within a complex organization.

ECB consists of the activities undertaken within an organization to make evaluation an ongoing, valued, and influential process. Extension evaluators have had a variety of experiences and successes in promoting ECB, and nationally it is an area of continuous activity in Extension programming.

Marc T. Braverman and Mary E. Arnold, in Chapter 6, discuss the challenges inherent in making decisions about methodological rigor. They analyze the costs and benefits of conducting rigorous evaluations, and they note that evaluators must keep in mind the specific evaluation context and information needs. The chapter examines how issues about methodology are linked to organizations' uses of evaluation, and how evaluators can influence this relationship.

In Chapter 7, Michael W. Duttweiler looks at the evaluation themes in action across a range of Extension programs. He presents data from the last ten years of the *Journal of Extension* to examine the functions that have been served by Extension evaluations and explores whether evaluations have made a tangible difference for Extension programs. He describes several cases in which evaluations have had a clear influence in changing program direction and promoting organizational learning.

Finally, in Chapter 8, Michael Quinn Patton takes a broad perspective relating the Extension experience to other organizational settings and evaluation practice in general. Presenting parallels between evaluation standards and principles of Extension work, he discusses the processes of organizational change as well as how organizations address the distinct evaluation purposes of accountability, program improvement, and knowledge generation. He also describes the lessons that Extension can offer about the situational appropriateness of methodological standards.

Taken together, the topics explored within this issue will be relevant to evaluators who operate in complex organizational environments with multiple stakeholders, organizational levels, organizational partners, and divergent purposes for evaluative information. The Extension system represents one of the largest arenas for using evaluation to shape social programs, and its experiences can contribute to a rapidly evolving knowledge base about effective evaluation practice across a variety of organizations.

References

Russ-Eft, D., & Preskill, H. (2001). *Evaluation in organizations: A systematic approach to enhancing learning, performance, and change.* Cambridge, MA: Perseus.

Sanders, J. R. (2002). Presidential address: On mainstreaming evaluation. *American Journal of Evaluation, 23*(3), 253–259.

Scheirer, M. A. (2005). Is sustainability possible? A review and commentary on empirical studies of program sustainability. *American Journal of Evaluation, 26*(3), 320–347.

Taut, S. (2007). Studying self-evaluation capacity building in a large international development organization. *American Journal of Evaluation, 28*(1), 45–59.

Torres, R. T., & Preskill, H. (2001). Evaluation and organizational learning: Past, present, and future. *American Journal of Evaluation, 22*(3), 387–395.

Marc T. Braverman
Molly Engle
Mary E. Arnold
Roger A. Rennekamp
Editors

MARC T. BRAVERMAN *is the associate dean for extension and outreach in the College of Health and Human Sciences, program leader of the Extension Family and Community Development Program, and a professor of human development and family sciences at Oregon State University.*

MOLLY ENGLE *is associate professor and Extension Service evaluation specialist at Oregon State University, and is a former president of the American Evaluation Association.*

MARY E. ARNOLD *is an associate professor and 4-H youth development specialist with the Oregon State University Extension Service, whose work involves teaching and conducting evaluations with the Oregon 4-H program.*

ROGER A. RENNEKAMP *is head of the Department of 4-H Youth Development Education at Oregon State University, and has also worked as a county Extension educator and state evaluation specialist.*

NEW DIRECTIONS FOR EVALUATION • DOI: 10.1002/ev

Franz, N. K., & Townson, L. (2008).The nature of complex organizations: The case of
Cooperative Extension. In M. T. Braverman, M. Engle, M. E. Arnold, & R. A. Rennekamp
(Eds.), *Program evaluation in a complex organizational system: Lessons from Cooperative
Extension. New Directions for Evaluation, 120*, 5–14.

1

The Nature of Complex Organizations: The Case of Cooperative Extension

Nancy K. Franz, Lisa Townson

Abstract

*The authors provide an overview of the Cooperative Extension System and its
program evaluation challenges. Part of the historic land-grant system, Extension exists in all states and territories of the United States and is funded through
federal, state, and local (usually county) appropriations, as well as competitive
grants and other sources. Complex funding, staffing, and accountability structures combined with widely varying programs and delivery methods make program development and evaluation challenging for Extension. Although each
state's Extension service operates autonomously, they all share a need to communicate program impacts and public value, which has become the main driver
for program evaluation. Further, organizational factors such as variation in program evaluation support across states, widely varied evaluation cultures, and
the grassroots nature of including stakeholders in program development add even
more complexity to evaluating Extension programs.* © Wiley Periodicals, Inc.

The Cooperative Extension System (CES), a land-grant university-
based outreach and educational organization, exists nationally in
every state and territory of the United States. Although most widely
known for the 4-H program, CES educators work in local municipalities as

an "extension" of the land-grant university, offering diverse educational programs in agriculture, community development, food and nutrition, youth development, and natural resources, making it the largest adult education organization in the United States (Griffith, 1991). Established in 1914, Cooperative Extension has local offices in more than 3,000 locations (typically county-based), with a common mission of supplying research-based information and education to people to help improve their lives. This large and complex educational organization affords a unique program evaluation context.

The Land-Grant University System

Although the Cooperative Extension System was established in 1914, the earlier creation of land-grant colleges set the stage for the existence of extended education. In 1862 President Lincoln signed the Morrill Act into law, granting land to each state, on the basis of the number of congressional seats held, to be used or sold to raise funds for a state land-grant college (Rasmussen, 1989). Then in 1890 the second Morrill Act gave states direct, annual federal appropriations to support their land-grant colleges and at the same time prohibit racial discrimination in admissions. At that time, 18 historically black colleges and universities were designated or formed, mostly across the South. Land-grant colleges were primarily designed to provide education and research in response to the needs of the agricultural community. In particular, 1890 land-grant colleges were charged with serving limited-resource audiences. This movement helped make the United States more competitive in agricultural and mechanical industries by not only teaching traditional students but welcoming farmers into classrooms and lectures to learn about new discoveries in agriculture and mechanization (Boyer, 1990).

Land-grant college leaders were concerned about future support of their colleges and agricultural experiment stations, and they realized that new discoveries and innovations needed to be accepted and implemented by farmers to make the societal contributions expected of them. The idea of "extension work" predates the legislation that created Cooperative Extension. When cotton fields across the South were threatened by the boll weevil in 1904, the U.S. Department of Agriculture deployed special "agents" (the term has been replaced by *educator* in many states) to work with farmers on their farms to combat the pest through demonstration-based education. In the decade that followed, several innovative experiments for taking university-based information to the people were launched. They included traveling workshops, moveable schools, and agricultural trains where university faculty would take their lectures and demonstrations out to communities (Reck, 1951). Research bulletins and leaflets became popular in disseminating information, but most were written for scholarly audiences, not the average farmer. Professors in some states began offering institutes at various locales during the winter to present their research to local farmers in a manner that was easily understood and applied. However, it soon became apparent that the most effective method of getting farmers to adopt changes was embedding university educators in local communities.

In 1914, the Smith-Lever Act allocated funds to land-grant universities, allowing them to place Extension educators in communities and on land-grant campuses all across America.[1] Extension educators worked initially in agriculture and later in home economics (now *family and consumer sciences*) and with 4-H clubs. Because these faculty and staff lived and worked among people in particular communities, they were in touch with local needs. Home economics educators began demonstrations as an effective educational model to help farm women improve food preparation and preservation, and to care for their homes and families. The most widely recognized Cooperative Extension program, 4-H, began early in the twentieth century. Educators found that teaching rural boys and girls new techniques such as use of hybrid seed corn and tomatoes was an effective way to get parents to adopt new technologies (Reck, 1951).

In 1994, the federal land-grant designation was also given to 33 American Indian colleges. This final designation brought to 108 the number of colleges and universities in the land-grant system. The Cooperative Extension designation makes these land-grant universities unique by adding specific responsibilities for outreach and service to the more widely recognized research and teaching functions of public universities.

Extension's Multifaceted Structure

The Cooperative Extension System is unique in its complex funding and accountability structure. Variations are found from state to state, but Figure 1.1 illustrates general CES staffing and funding based on a four-part partnership.

County and municipal governments provide funding and other support for local offices, including partial salary coverage for local Extension educators. State government supplies fiscal support for educators in local units and on land-grant campuses and agricultural research stations. The federal government, through the U.S. Department of Agriculture's Cooperative State Research, Education, and Extension Service,[2] also provides funding for a portion of Extension salaries and operations (Apps, 2002). Changes in local, county, and federal fiscal support for Extension are moderated by funding through grants, contracts, fiscal gifts, and user fees (Franz, 2002). Traditionally, for example, funding for Cooperative Extension was one-third federal funding, one-third state funding, and one-third county or local funding. Today, these portions can range from 10% to 70% for each partner. Budgets and fiscal sources can vary greatly from location to location. For example, one county in rural Wisconsin receives approximately $200,000 to conduct extension programs while an urban New York county receives more than $1 million for its extension work.

NEW DIRECTIONS FOR EVALUATION • DOI: 10.1002/ev

Figure 1.1. The Cooperative Extension System Partnership

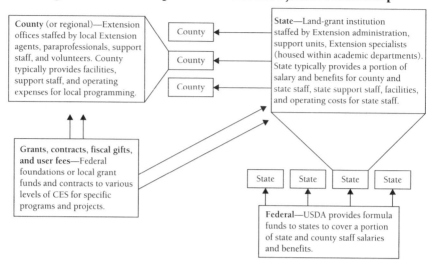

At each land-grant college or university, Extension is located in a col-lege of agriculture, or in another college, or as part of two or more colleges, or it stands alone as an academic unit outside a college. At the University of New Hampshire, Cooperative Extension is a stand-alone unit, with a dean who reports directly to the provost; at Virginia Polytechnic Institute and State University, Extension is housed within the College of Agriculture and Life Sciences. In Wisconsin, Cooperative Extension falls under a broader outreach unit that also includes public television and radio and con-tinuing education; Extension faculty are located in a variety of colleges at the main campus in Madison as well as other UW campuses across the state.

Extension's Staffing

State Extension units are administered by academic officials located at land-grant university campuses and in district or regional offices in each state. Extension educators housed within campus academic departments or at campus research centers are typically responsible for coordinating needs assessment and program development, leading program-related research projects, and furnishing subject matter expertise to support educational pro-grams. An educator also may work with Extension program evaluators to develop evaluation plans and tools for statewide educational programs.

County, multicounty, or multistate Extension educators housed in local offices plan, implement, and evaluate educational experiences for their clientele. Staffing varies considerably from location to location according to local needs and available funding. For example, in New York City 70 staff conduct programs on the urban environment, nutrition, health, families,

NEW DIRECTIONS FOR EVALUATION • DOI: 10.1002/ev

and youth. On the other hand, some rural offices may have only a single 4-H educator in residence, with visiting agriculture or family and consumer science educators from other offices making farm visits, conducting workshops, and answering questions for clientele.

Finally, Extension recruits, trains, and uses hundreds of thousands of volunteers to help plan, deliver, and evaluate extension educational programs (Seevers, Graham, & Conklin, 2007). Volunteers serve in a variety of roles, among them as local advisory councils, Master Gardeners,[3] and 4-H leaders.

Cooperative Extension Programs

Historically, Extension has concentrated on three programmatic foci: agriculture, home economics, and 4-H with rural audiences. As U.S. demographics have changed, so has the programming of Cooperative Extension. Program areas now include agriculture and natural resources, family and consumer sciences, 4-H youth development, and community development. Although production agriculture remains an important component, programs now include a focus on practices that protect the environment. Today, diverse educational programs are offered for families and communities on topics such as nutrition and food safety, financial management, parenting, community and economic development, and water quality. In Ohio, Extension addresses current economic issues by helping families facing foreclosure through online tools and a home study course on money management and strategies for surviving financial crisis (Ohio State University Extension, 2008).

4-H programs are now available for a variety of youth from urban, rural, and suburban locations with diverse interests. Project work ranges from aerospace to electricity, animals, nutrition and wellness, and computer technology. Rural audiences are still served, but Extension's clientele are increasingly urban and periurban. Extension is increasingly involved with more complex economic, environmental, and social issues (Seevers et al., 2007). The Rural Bridges program in Washington state works with communities and industry to expand jobs and improve local economies through innovative uses of information technology (Washington State University, 2007). Further, in most states Extension programs target limited-income families with nutrition education for those receiving state and federal aid. Many state Extension programs also offer youth development activities for low-income communities in after-school settings focused on life skill development. Other programs offer parenting training for prison inmates.

Program Partnerships

Extension educators rarely plan, conduct, and evaluate educational work in isolation. To the contrary, they often build extensive partnerships and

10 PROGRAM EVALUATION IN A COMPLEX ORGANIZATIONAL SYSTEM

collaborations with government, nongovernmental organizations (NGOs), and other groups to deepen and broaden the impact of their efforts (Franz, 2003). In Florida, Extension partners with the Florida Department of Environmental Protection and the Southwest Florida Water Management District to offer information and programs on Florida-friendly landscaping (University of Florida, 2008). In other states, horticulture educators work with the green industry, public agencies, volunteers, homeowners' associations, and turf managers on programs to reduce water pollution through decreased fertilizer application and other practices. Family and consumer science educators work with social services, churches, schools, and non-profit organizations to offer parenting programs. In Virginia, 4-H educators work with schools, health departments, hospitals, and civic clubs to address youth obesity in their communities through in-school programs, after-school programs, camps, and community fairs.

Approaches to Extension Work

As Figure 1.2 illustrates, Extension educators approach their work in a variety of ways. This model, created by Merrill Ewert, a past director of Cornell Cooperative Extension, focuses on two dimensions: process and content (Franz, 2002). *Process* refers to the methods used to deliver educational programs, and *content* refers to the information shared that helps change learners' knowledge or behavior. Combining these dimensions presents four domains that describe how extension work is conducted.

The first domain, "service," includes functions conducted by Extension educators that range from soil testing and pressure canner testing to forming and serving on community committees and task forces. Educators using this approach offer low levels of process and content in delivering these services but find the work important for building relationships with clientele groups and addressing basic clientele needs.

Figure 1.2. Extension Educational Approaches

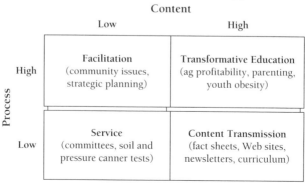

The "facilitation" approach finds Extension educators serving as facilitators of group process in educational settings rather than delivering information directly. Educators using this approach excel at bringing a variety of voices to the table to solve multifaceted problems using a number of techniques. Extension educators often facilitate public forums on community issues or strategic planning sessions for nonprofit organizations.

Extension educators are historically known for bringing land-grant research-based information to individuals, communities, and businesses through the third approach, "content transmission." This approach includes creation of fact sheets, curriculum, newsletters, articles, Web sites, Power-Point presentations, and other resources to address ongoing and emerging issues. Clientele access this information directly or through local Extension educators. Educators also create and disseminate localized content to supplement statewide or regional information.

The final approach to extension work, "transformative education," happens when Extension educators develop long-term educational relationships with clientele to focus on changes in their learning and behavior. This in turn leads to change in social, environmental, and economic conditions (Franz, 2002). These programs are intentionally designed to work with audiences over time rather than through single educational events. This allows learners to gain new competencies, apply what they've learned to their personal context, share results with each other, and adjust their application of learning as needed. This approach to extension work is often highlighted in documenting the value of Cooperative Extension to the public.

One example of transformative education is an agricultural profitability program where the educator works in a community with farmers who are struggling to survive economically. The educator develops a comprehensive program to deliver information and educational processes on best practices through publications, demonstrations, meetings, Web-based information, field days, farm visits, news articles, and more. This effort requires a long-term, in-depth educational relationship with the farmers. In another example of transformative education, 4-H youth development educators conduct programs over many years that develop leadership skills in adults and youths through 4-H clubs, contests, camps, and other delivery methods. Finally, family and consumer science educators help transform communities and individuals over time through in-depth parenting programs that change parent and child behavior through group discussion, presentations, individual counseling, Web-based information, news articles, and trying new parenting techniques in a supportive environment.

Program Development Model

In addition to educational approaches to extension work, a relatively consistent program development model is used for educational programming by

Cooperative Extension across land-grant universities. Extension programming rests on a base of grassroots involvement. Educators infuse feedback from clients, advisory councils, and other stakeholder groups into programming (Buford, Bedeian, & Lindner, 1995). This program development model's basic elements include (1) situation analysis, (2) program design and implementation, and (3) program evaluation and reporting. In the first step, Extension educators work with stakeholders to scan the environment and determine issues and needs to be addressed by Extension. Most local and state Extension units work with volunteer advisory groups that assist with this process. Educators then collaborate with stakeholders to create and carry out programs. Finally, educators and stakeholders determine the level of success realized from these educational efforts through program evaluation and reporting.

Organizational Factors Influencing Evaluation in Extension

The organizational complexity of Extension constitutes a rich context in which to explore factors that influence the success of program evaluation efforts. For example, consider the following:

- The main driver for program evaluation in Cooperative Extension is public accountability to maintain and increase funding. With its reliance on multiple funding streams from local, state, federal, and nongovernmental sources, Extension strives to tell the story of program impact and public value to a variety of audiences. This process becomes increasingly critical as competition for public funding rises and as economic, environmental, and social issues become more complex. In addition, the variety of fiscal and programmatic timelines prescribed by funders can present challenges for coordination of data collection and reporting.
- Cooperative Extension has a variety of levels of operation: community, county, regional, state, multistate, and national. An understanding of how the organization functions at each level, as well as across levels, is needed to make program evaluation efforts useful and relevant.
- Evaluation staffing and support differ by state and are organized in a variety of ways. Some states lend little support for program evaluation, even in cases where they place a strong organizational focus on program impact. In these instances, local audiences and educators may see evaluation as unnecessary or an "add-on" to programming. In other states, Extension educators operate as evaluation practitioners supported by a cadre of professionally trained evaluators. In all instances, additional support is needed to build the capacity of educators to conduct program evaluation and to direct resources to hire external evaluators when the occasion demands.

NEW DIRECTIONS FOR EVALUATION • DOI: 10.1002/ev

- Cooperative Extension educators across the country have a high degree of autonomy in planning, implementing, and evaluating their educational programming. Their efforts may include statewide or regional programming but may also be local and context-specific. Educators value this autonomy, but it sometimes creates challenges for building educator evaluation capacity and may make collecting multisite evaluation data difficult.
- Cooperative Extension addresses an array of stakeholder interests in educational programs and outcomes. This can result in differing goals among partners who sponsor and work with Extension programs. Consistent with Extension's strong volunteer base and grassroots focus on programming, stakeholders are often involved in program evaluation efforts. Their participation may include evaluation planning, data collection, data analysis, and reporting results. The involvement of stakeholders in program evaluation has become increasingly important as Extension educators broaden and deepen their programming efforts, but it may also present challenges for coordination of activities.
- The Extension evaluation culture often uses limited evaluation methodologies. Postsurveys of educational activities are common, but focus groups, interviews, observations, and analysis of secondary data are much less frequent. Use of control groups is rare. The focus of program evaluation efforts can involve performance, program, and product improvement, but evidence of Extension's ability to effect positive environmental, economic, and social change is currently given greatest emphasis.

Summary

The Cooperative Extension System addresses public needs through community-based educational programs. The organization has grown to become the largest adult education organization in the United States, with multifaceted structures and staffing patterns, a variety of programs and program partnerships, and diverse educational approaches. These organizational factors have become more complex over time, increasing the importance of program evaluation for communicating Cooperative Extension's public value, understanding its programs, and continuing its sustainability. Further chapters in this issue address how Cooperative Extension deals with program evaluation within this complex environment.

Notes

1. Extension educators hold a variety of titles across the nation, including but not limited to agent, associate, program assistant, faculty, and specialist.
2. The 2008 Farm Bill passed by Congress calls for a reorganization of the U.S. Department of Agriculture's Cooperative State Research, Education, and Extension Service

(CSREES), the agency that is Cooperative Extension's federal partner. As this issue goes to press, the plan calls for the new agency name to become the National Institute of Food and Agriculture, with the reorganization to be effective by October 2009.

3. Master volunteers usually receive in-depth training of at least 40 hours and are required to give at least 40 hours of public service in return.

References

Apps, J. (2002). *The people came first: A history of Wisconsin Cooperative Extension.* Madison, WI: Epsilon Sigma Phi Foundation.

Boyer, E. L. (1990). *Scholarship reconsidered: Priorities of the professorate.* New York: Carnegie Foundation.

Buford, J., Bedeian, A., & Lindner, J. (1995). *Management in Extension* (3rd ed.). Columbus: Ohio State University Extension.

Franz, N. (2002). *Transformative learning in intraorganizational partnerships.* Unpublished doctoral dissertation, Cornell University, Ithaca, NY.

Franz, N. (2003). Transformative learning in Extension staff partnerships: Facilitating personal, joint, and organizational change. *Journal of Extension, 41*(2). Retrieved October 29, 2007, from http://www.joe.org/joe/2003april/a1.shtml

Griffith, W. (1991). The impact of intellectual leadership. In J. Peters & P. Jarvis (Eds.), *Adult education: Evolution and achievements in a developing field of study* (pp. 97–120). San Francisco: Jossey-Bass.

Ohio State University Extension (2008). *OSU Extension offers tools for Ohioans facing foreclosure.* Retrieved February 6, 2008, from http://extension.osu.edu/~news/story.php?id=4462

Rasmussen, W. (1989). *Taking the university to the people: Seventy-five years of Cooperative Extension.* Ames: Iowa State University Press.

Reck, F. M. (1951). *The 4-H story: A history of 4-H club work.* Ames: Iowa State College Press.

Seevers, B., Graham, D., & Conklin, N. (2007). *Education through Cooperative Extension* (2nd ed.). Columbus: The Ohio State University.

University of Florida. (2008). *UF/IFAS Extension solutions for your life.* Retrieved February 11, 2008, from http://extension.ifas.ufl.edu/lawn_and_garden/

Washington State University. (2007). *Community development.* Retrieved February 2, 2008, from http://ext.wsu.edu/economicbenefits/community-development.html

NANCY K. FRANZ *is a professor and Extension specialist, program development, with Virginia Cooperative Extension at Virginia Polytechnic Institute and State University in the Department of Agricultural and Extension Education, and she formerly worked with Cooperative Extension in New Hampshire, New York, and Wisconsin as an agent, specialist, administrative coordinator, and administrator.*

LISA TOWNSON *is an Extension specialist in program development and evaluation for the University of New Hampshire Cooperative Extension.*

NEW DIRECTIONS FOR EVALUATION • DOI: 10.1002/ev

Rennekamp, R. A., & Engle, M. (2008). A case study in organizational change: Evaluation in Cooperative Extension. In M. T. Braverman, M. Engle, M. E. Arnold, & R. A. Rennekamp (Eds.), *Program evaluation in a complex organizational system: Lessons from Cooperative Extension. New Directions for Evaluation, 120*, 15–26.

2

A Case Study in Organizational Change: Evaluation in Cooperative Extension

Roger A. Rennekamp, Molly Engle

Abstract

This chapter examines how factors both internal and external to Cooperative Extension have influenced its commitment and capability to assess the quality and impact of its programs. The authors begin by documenting how the nature of Extension programming has changed dramatically in response to societal needs over the course of the organization's history. Because Extension's culture places great value on service to people, early attempts to measure organizational performance focused on the number of individuals reached and the quality of the interaction with those individuals. Over time, Extension educators began to turn their attention to program outcomes. But it wasn't until Extension was threatened with significant budget cuts that the organization responded with systemwide efforts to document the results of its programming. The authors conclude that so long as Extension educators consider program evaluation an obligation to be met rather than an opportunity to learn and grow, optimum levels of commitment and capability cannot be achieved. © Wiley Periodicals, Inc.

As a highly decentralized and widely distributed system, Cooperative Extension presents the evaluation community with an intriguing case for examining the growth of evaluation capacity within an organization over a span of nearly a hundred years. This chapter examines how

factors both internal and external to Cooperative Extension have influenced its commitment and capability to assess the quality and impact of its programs.

Established in 1914 by the Smith-Lever Act, Cooperative Extension serves as the educational outreach network of the nation's land-grant universities and federal Department of Agriculture. Because these land-grant universities originated as agriculture and mechanics colleges designed to reach the working classes, the nature of their outreach was decidedly focused on agriculture. Over the years, however, Extension programming has diversified significantly to address the ever-changing needs of society. Consequently, we begin our examination of Cooperative Extension with a look at the responsive and dynamic nature of Extension programming.

Programmatic Diversity

Extension programs respond to local needs and issues. As a result, the focus of Extension work differs from state to state and county to county. As needs and issues change, programs evolve to meet those needs. But even in its early years, responding to the complex issues of a rural agrarian population required significant programmatic diversity. A 1923 annual report of the Kentucky Cooperative Extension Service cited by Smith (1981) summarized the broad array of issues facing these early Extension workers:

> Contrary to what one might think, it is fact that the average Kentucky farmer does not yet take care to test the seed he plants; he still feeds rations that are far from best for his stock. The livestock are of such quality that they can never hope to reach the top of the market. The cows he feeds are such low producers that milk is produced at an unnecessarily high cost. He does not know which of his hens in the poultry flock are good layers and which are not. He keeps no cost accounts or records of the year's business. He works too hard in the summer and not enough in the winter. He takes very poor care of farm machinery, and only recently is beginning to dispose of even a portion of his products in a thoroughly businesslike way. (p. 252)

Addressing the many needs and issues of farmers through responsive programming was indeed a challenge for early Extension workers. These educators developed a "listen and respond" approach to programming. The predominant methods used by early Extension educators were individual consultation and field demonstration.

Parallel to the work with farmers was programming designed to reach rural families and youths. Home demonstration agents helped rural women learn to cook, sew, preserve food, and manage resources. 4-H youth programs of Cooperative Extension grew and expanded (Wessel & Wessel, 1982). But for the first half of its existence, Extension programming still reflected strong ties to its agricultural roots, with only minor efforts directed toward new audiences and issues (Seevers, Graham, & Conklin, 2007).

By the 1960s, demographic shifts in the nation's population made it difficult for Extension to serve only rural and agricultural audiences. Extension responded quickly with a wave of programs aimed at reaching urban and suburban audiences. Still, critics felt that Cooperative Extension had outlived its usefulness. Others, conversely, called for land-grant institutions across the nation to renew their commitment to community engagement, but with the nimbleness needed to respond to a wider array of community issues (Kellogg Commission, 1999). Consequently, the scope of Cooperative Extension work began to broaden at an accelerated rate. New programs addressed obesity, physical activity, technological literacy, aging, watershed management, sustainable energy, workforce development, and emergency preparedness.

One could argue that situational responsiveness is a valid indicator of organizational performance. But how would Extension workers choose to measure the performance of individual programs? At least in its early years, Extension workers made significant efforts to document program reach and the quality of relationships with clients.

Reach and Relationships

Early accomplishment reports by Extension workers tended to focus on the expanded reach of Extension, as an increasing number of agents were placed in rural communities across America. Some tried to capture the results of their work in reports they submitted to their universities. One agent, based in Umatilla County, Oregon, glowingly reflected on his accomplishments in the area of poultry production in his 1923 annual report (Ballard, 1961):

> Largely as a result of work on demonstration farms, newspaper publicity, and talks advocating increases in commercial poultry raising in districts of the county adapted to the same, the number of farms on which poultry is made a regular part of the farm business with at least 200 hens, increased from two farms with 1,175 hens in 1921 to 56 farms with 19,250 hens in 1923. Fourteen poultry meetings were held and attended by 327 people. (p. 435)

Some agents' accounts of their work were colorful and rich in detail. Describing his pioneer work in Missouri, an early Extension worker recalled:

> One of the county officials was antagonistic to [Extension] work and wouldn't have anything to do with me. But to my surprise, one afternoon he walked into my office and asked "Do you know anything about watermelons?" I suggested that we go to his field, where I showed him techniques such as finding

the dead tendril stem, thumping to note the dead rather than metallic sound, pushing the melon to get a crushing sound, and the yellow color on the bottom. I told him to plug the melon and it came out a nice red color. Not convinced, he had me select two others which both proved ripe. "Well," he said, "I guess you do know something I don't." He was a loyal supporter of my work from that day. (Reeder, 1979, p. 7)

There are many plausible explanations for such a heavy focus on reach and relationships in evaluating early Extension programs. Some have suggested that because Extension workers are embedded within communities and serve with a mission of outreach, a desire to speak of the breadth and quality of their contacts with community members is quite natural. Others believe that civil rights and affirmative action legislation reinforces a "counting culture" within the organization. Still others suggest that it was the absence of meaningful program plans and measurable program goals or objectives that reinforced documentation of reach and relationships (Warner & Christenson, 1984).

Customer Satisfaction

A national assessment of Cooperative Extension by Warner and Christenson (1984) offered the first systematic look at the public's perception of Extension. Specifically this study examined awareness of Cooperative Extension by the general population, user satisfaction with its services, and the public's willingness to fund Cooperative Extension programs.

According to those authors, approximately 40% of the population recognized the Cooperative Extension Service by name. Recognition of individual Extension programs such as 4-H was dramatically higher. As one might expect, those most aware of Cooperative Extension and its programs were older, white, more affluent residents of rural areas. Among users nationwide, more than 90% were satisfied with the services they had received from Cooperative Extension. The more satisfied that users were with the services, the more willing they were to support continued or increased appropriations for Cooperative Extension.

In 1993, the Government Performance and Results Act (GPRA) required all federal agencies to develop measurable performance objectives as a part of the budget process. This resulted in an expectation that continued funding to each agency would be contingent on its achievement of those performance objectives. There was considerable variation in the nature of the performance objectives selected by numerous agencies, making it difficult to compare their relative effectiveness.

Several years later, a number of state governments implemented performance-based budgeting initiatives similar to GPRA. Although some states negotiated performance objectives with individual agencies, others chose to use standard measures for determining performance. For example, the

Florida legislature required all public agencies to conduct annual measures of customer satisfaction. Through their annual assessment, Florida Cooperative Extension determined that 98% of Extension clients in their state were either satisfied or very satisfied with the quality of service received (Terry & Israel, 2004). Other studies of customer satisfaction with Cooperative Extension have produced similarly high satisfaction rates.

Compared with other government agencies, Extension's customer satisfaction scores appeared quite good. Consequently, Extension administrators were more than willing to use customer satisfaction scores as an indicator of performance, particularly if a high level of satisfaction were tied to funding. Measuring customer satisfaction was also considerably less difficult than measuring program outcomes or impacts, particularly those that may not be realized until some time in the future.

Efforts to measure customer satisfaction constituted limited evidence of program effectiveness, but they were highly instrumental in preparing Extension staff to conduct more sophisticated evaluations. Eventually, Extension field staff began to add questions related to learning and the intent to change behavior to simple end-of-meeting questionnaires, which previously focused only on collecting client reactions to their experience with Extension.

Learning and Behavior Change

Until the 1950s, Extension workers paid little attention to the human processes underlying learning and behavioral change. Over the next several decades, however, all of that changed.

Benjamin Bloom's (1956) taxonomy of educational objectives helped Extension staff understand how learners apply knowledge and assign meaning to learning. Malcolm Knowles's (1960) seminal work in adult education had long-lasting influence on the field of Extension education, helping practitioners tailor programs to the unique characteristics of adult learners. Mager's (1962) work in the area of preparing instructional objectives helped Extension faculty and staff give intentional thought to what they hoped would happen as a result of instruction. Later, Kolb and Fry's (1975) work in experiential learning furnished a framework for applying the popularized learn-by-doing approach of 4-H to broader Extension work.

Work in the area of human behavior in social systems was equally influential. Beal and Bohlen (1955) introduced a model by which change agents could apply knowledge of the social sciences through a purposeful process of initiating and supporting behavioral change. Everett Rogers (1962, 1983) further postulated that the rate at which individuals adopt innovations is variable and influenced by a number of factors. Together, these two models helped to formalize thinking about the process of behavioral change and served for many years as the predominant theories of change guiding Extension's agricultural programs.

But they were not the only models used by Cooperative Extension for thinking about learning, growth, and change. Extension's family and youth development programs were influenced by several complementary theories of behavioral change. For example, Prochaska and DiClemente's (1986) Transtheoretical Model also attempts to explain the process of behavioral change. Unlike Rogers, Prochaska and DiClemente based their model on many years of empirical research into how effective interventions promote health behavior change, specifically addictive behaviors. The Transtheoretical Model suggests that changes in health behavior unfold through five clear and distinct stages: precontemplation, contemplation, preparation, action, and maintenance of the change. The model also considered the effects of psychological, environmental, cultural, socioeconomic, physiological, biochemical, and genetic variables, all of which may affect behavior.

The previously mentioned change theories acknowledge that numerous environmental factors affect behavioral change, but none does so as strongly as the ecological systems theory of Bronfenbrenner (1979). Systems theory views individuals as organisms in a particular environment. It suggests that there are bidirectional relationships between the individual and the various elements of that environment. Behavioral change, therefore, is influenced not only by the attributes and mental processes of an individual but by elements of the external environment as well.

The lasting impact of these works has been to entrench behavioral change as a logical and valued outcome of Extension programming, particularly in areas of work where social, economic, or environmental benefits may be deferred or difficult to measure.

Beyond Behavioral Change

Perhaps the most important contributor to the advancement of evaluative thought within Cooperative Extension was Claude Bennett, a long-time evaluation specialist with the U.S. Department of Agriculture. His results hierarchy (Bennett, 1975) introduced Extension workers to a hierarchy of program accomplishments and outcomes that culminated with the desired changes in social, economic, or environmental conditions to be brought about by the program.

Bennett's hierarchy gave Extension educators a generic framework for thinking about the results of their programs. As described by Bennett (1975):

> First in the chain are inputs, the resources expended by Extension. These inputs produce activities which involve people who have reactions, pro and con. People involved may change knowledge, attitudes, skills, or aspirations (KASA). Practice change occurs when people apply their KASA change to working or living. What follows from these practice changes are end results. Such results should include the ultimate aims of the Extension program. (p. 7)

Perhaps the most significant benefit of Bennett's work was that it helped Extension workers think simultaneously about various types of program outcomes. Admittedly, Bennett's hierarchy was initially used by Extension staff as a scheme for categorizing the level of outcome measured, rather than as a tool for developing a theory of change, but his subsequent work with Kay Rockwell at the University of Nebraska (Bennett & Rockwell, 1995) resulted in an advanced model with increased utility as a planning tool.

In the revised model, programmers are encouraged to start the program planning process by first articulating the ultimate aims of the program. They then identify the changes in behavior that would produce the desired results, continuing to work backward until the resources needed for implementation are identified. What Bennett and Rockwell (1995) created was in essence a framework by which Extension staff could build logic models for their programs.

Logic Modeling in Extension

Simply stated, a logic model is a picture of how a program is supposed to operate (Wholey, 1979). Logic models specify the chain of actions, events, or outcomes that a program intends to set in motion. The relationships between elements in the chain are presented as "if-then" relationships (United Way of America, 1996). Assertions about these relationships are based on research, experience, intuition, and other sources of knowledge. Logic models help to make the theory behind a program explicit. Some logic models are simple linear chains; others are more complex and systems-oriented. There is no prescribed formula for how a finished model should look, but the benefits of using logic models in program development are clear and compelling.

The W. K. Kellogg Foundation (2004) cites several benefits of using logic models in program development. First, logic models serve as a guide for program planning, a blueprint for implementation, and a framework for evaluation. Second, logic models can help us communicate our plans to others who may be contemplating an initial or continuing investment in that program. Third, logic models reflect a shared understanding of a program that results from facilitated dialogue among members of the design team. Finally, logic models serve as diagnostic tools to help us figure out why programs are not working as planned.

The idea of communicating the rationale for a program in a clear and compelling fashion is not necessarily new to Extension, however. Taylor, Summerhill, and Taylor (1983) argued for such as they advocated for additional "preprogram accountability":

> Extension agents are increasingly finding themselves in situations where, as a basis for funding, key decision makers are demanding that we provide a defensible program rationale and evidence of planning that would indicate

a high degree of assurance of accomplishment. To effectively meet the pre-program accountability challenge, we must develop a logical, concise program rationale that provides a clear picture of clientele needs and assurances that the program will address that need and accomplish its intended mission. (p. 64)

In 1996, the Kentucky Cooperative Extension Service embedded a logic model framework in its electronic planning and reporting system. Extension faculty and staff were asked to identify long-term, intermediate, and initial outcomes for each major program. They then identified the learning experiences that were to produce those outcomes as well as the evaluation procedures and protocols they would use to measure program outcomes. In the late nineties, several Extension evaluators began to advocate for broader usage of logic models in Extension program design (Rennekamp, 1997).

A team at the University of Wisconsin–Cooperative Extension, led by Ellen Taylor-Powell, popularized logic modeling across Extension with an easy-to-use framework that was adopted by many states as their program planning model and with online tools specifically for Extension educators (see Chapter Five by Taylor-Powell and Boyd). The Cooperative State Research, Education, and Extension Service (CSREES)[1] used logic modeling for the first time in fiscal year 2007. Major efforts are currently under way throughout the Cooperative Extension System to help build understanding and use of program logic models.

A Call to Action

Without question, the 1980s marked a new era for program evaluation in Cooperative Extension. Andrews (1983) summarized this new environment by writing:

No longer can it be taken for granted that programs are good and appropriate. Extension is operating in a new environment—an environment of more open criticism and demands for justification of actions. All publicly funded agencies, not just Extension, are vulnerable in these times. In an era of accountability, Extension must be able to defend who and how people are being served. It also needs to document that programs are achieving positive results. (p. 8)

Some argued that this call for increased accountability was not without warning. The Food and Agriculture Act of 1977 instructed the secretary of agriculture to conduct an evaluation of the social and economic impacts of Cooperative Extension programs. The report of that effort, released in 1980, found Cooperative Extension's accountability work to be "short on impacts" and "long on documenting participation and activity levels of programs" (Warner & Christenson, 1984, p. 17).

The Extension Committee on Organization and Policy (ECOP) responded by appointing a national task force on accountability and evaluation in Cooperative Extension. The report of the task force called for systemwide accomplishment data augmented by evaluations of select, high-priority programs. It also called for more detailed information on participants and the resources used to reach them. In addition, it recommended creation of a national staff to impart leadership to planning and accountability (National Task Force, 1981).

Also in 1981, an assessment of Cooperative Extension issued by the General Accounting Office (GAO) criticized it for not having a clearly defined focus. Further troubling to the GAO was Extension's inability to demonstrate the results of the programs it did conduct. Specifically, the report cited the need for improved evaluation and accountability in Extension (United States General Accounting Office, 1981).

Late in 1983, a special issue of the *Journal of Extension* focused on program evaluation. In those articles, leading Extension evaluators focused on topics ranging from methodology to communication of evaluation results.

In addition, the Agricultural Research, Extension, and Education Reform Act (AREERA) of 1998 required state Extension services to document the amount of federal funds being dedicated to multistate projects as well as to those with significant links to land-grant research initiatives.

Leadership to Evaluation and Accountability

Beginning in the 1980s, Extension specialists focusing on program evaluation began to appear with greater frequency across the Extension system. Many of these evaluators were given the nebulous charge of helping to make Extension more accountable, while some gave leadership to clearly defined evaluations of statewide programs. Others focused their efforts on building the capacity of Extension faculty to conduct their own evaluations.

The leadership for these efforts arose from the social science units associated with Extension work, most notably community development, rural sociology, and agricultural economics. Consequently, an evaluation research paradigm arose across Extension, characterized by application of social science research methods to answer practical questions about program quality and results. Over time, Extension evaluators with disciplinary backgrounds in other fields became more commonplace. Many of the early Extension evaluators, notably Claude Bennett, Michael Patton, and Richard Krueger, went on to have significant influence on the evaluation community.

The emergence of leadership for program evaluation and accountability within Cooperative Extension roughly paralleled the emergence of evaluation as a field. Currently, the Extension Education Evaluation Topical Interest Group (EEE-TIG) of the American Evaluation Association presents a forum for Extension evaluators to address issues of practice.

Several current proposals for system reform at the federal level reflect an increasing emphasis on competitive funding for new Extension projects, in contrast to historical reliance on formula funding for determining each state's appropriation. Competitive funding landscapes demand greater focus on sound program design as well as demonstrated capacity to measure program results.

Analysis

The purpose of this chapter has been to examine how factors both internal and external to Cooperative Extension influenced its commitment and capability to assess the quality and impact of its programs. From this description of Cooperative Extension, the authors offer three key observations that may prove beneficial to others examining change in a large organization.

First, it is clear that across Cooperative Extension increased commitment to evaluation has been driven by *external pressure* to demonstrate results or ensure program quality. Unfortunately, evaluation is still too often viewed as the process that produces data for accountability reports. Perhaps this is a natural phenomenon in large organizations, particularly those that pride themselves on service to people. This dedication to service has frequently been likened to a "calling" that brings people to Extension work. Many Extension workers simply believe that time spent on program evaluation is time that could be better spent serving people. But because of Extension's ties to academia, one could logically expect a stronger culture of inquiry to be prevalent across Cooperative Extension.

Second, the capability to assess the quality and impact of programs is largely driven by *internal decisions* initiated by the organization. Seeing the need to build evaluation capacity across the system, Extension administrators have bolstered support to the evaluation function of the organization. Consequently, the number of evaluation specialists in the Extension system has grown rapidly over the past 20 years. With connections to the broader evaluation community, Extension evaluators optimize best practices from the field for use in Extension contexts. Extension evaluation specialists serve as consultants, coaches, and trainers of local Extension educators. In addition to capacity building, many of these specialists regularly conduct evaluations on behalf of the organization.

Finally, the success of these organizational interventions is moderated by *program maturity*. As a program matures, individuals involved with it develop a more sophisticated understanding of how the program goes about achieving its objectives. Similarly, the underlying program theory becomes more mature as assumptions and beliefs about the program are confirmed or dispelled. Such understandings produce higher-order thought about what should be measured. If a mature program theory is lacking, surrogate indicators of program performance, such as participant satisfaction with educators' work, often take the place of more meaningful measures of program outcomes.

The evolution of commitment and capacity for program evaluation in the Cooperative Extension System has been neither rudderless nor strategic, neither random nor calculated. When the relevance, quality, or impacts of Extension programs are called into question, Extension educators deliver. Their unwavering belief in the merits of their work drives them to respond with vigor to calls for greater accountability. They seek opportunities to polish their evaluation skills and respond to the challenge. But optimum levels of evaluation commitment and capacity will be achieved only if the commitment is driven by a desire to learn and grow from the results of systematic inquiry.

Note

1. The 2008 Farm Bill passed by Congress calls for a reorganization of the U.S. Department of Agriculture's Cooperative State Research, Education, and Extension Service (CSREES), the agency that is Cooperative Extension's federal partner. As this issue goes to press, the plan calls for the new agency name to become the National Institute of Food and Agriculture, with the reorganization to be effective by October 2009.

References

Andrews, M. (1983). Evaluation: An essential process. *Journal of Extension, 21*(5), 8–13.

Ballard, F. L. (1961). *The Oregon State University Federal Cooperative Extension Service.* Corvallis: Oregon State University.

Beal, G. M., & Bohlen, J. M. (1955). *How farm people accept new ideas* (Cooperative Extension Service Report 15). Ames, IA: Department of Agriculture.

Bennett, C. (1975). Up the hierarchy. *Journal of Extension, 13*(2), 7–12.

Bennett, C., & Rockwell, K. (1995). *Targeting outcomes of programs (TOP): An integrated approach to planning and evaluation.* Retrieved April 1, 2008, from http://citnews.unl.edu/TOP/english/index.html

Bloom, B. S. (Ed.). (1956). *Taxonomy of educational objectives: The classification of educational goals.* New York: McKay.

Bronfenbrenner, U. (1979). *The ecology of human development: Experiments by nature and design.* Cambridge, MA: Harvard University Press.

Kellogg Commission on the Future of State and Land-Grant Universities. (1999). *Returning to our roots: The engaged institution.* Washington, DC: National Association of State Universities and Land-Grant Colleges.

Knowles, M. S. (Ed.) (1960). *Handbook of adult education in the United States.* Chicago: Adult Education Association of the USA.

Kolb, D., & Fry, R. (1975). Towards an applied theory of experiential learning. In C. L. Cooper (Ed.), *Theories of group processes* (pp. 33–58). London: Wiley.

Mager, R. F. (1962). *Preparing objectives for programmed instruction.* Belmont, CA: David S. Lake.

National Task Force on the Extension Accountability and Evaluation System. (1981). *Report of the National Task Force on the Extension Accountability and Evaluation.* Morgantown: West Virginia University, Cooperative Extension Service.

Prochaska, J. O., & DiClemente, C. C. (1986). Toward a comprehensive model of change. In W. R. Miller and N. Heather (Eds.), *Treating addictive behaviors: Processes of change* (pp. 3–28). New York: Plenum.

Reeder, R. L. (1979). *The people and the profession: Selected memories of veteran Extension workers.* National Board of Epsilon Sigma Phi.

Rennekamp, R. (1997, November). *Building linkages and solving mysteries: Using logic models in program development.* Paper presented at the annual meeting of the American Evaluation Association, San Diego, CA.

Rogers, E. M. (1962). *Diffusion of innovations.* New York: Free Press.

Rogers, E. M. (1983). *Diffusion of innovations* (3rd ed.). New York: Free Press.

Seevers, B., Graham, D., & Conklin, N. (2007). *Education through Cooperative Extension* (2nd ed.). Columbus: The Ohio State University.

Smith, J. A. (1981). *The College of Agriculture of the University of Kentucky.* Lexington: Kentucky Agricultural Experiment Station.

Taylor, B., Summerhill, B., & Taylor, C. (1983). Meeting the accountability challenge. *Journal of Extension, 21*(5), 64–65.

Terry, B. D., & Israel, G. D. (2004). Agent performance and customer satisfaction. *Journal of Extension, 42*(6). Retrieved March 1, 2008, from http://www.joe.org/joe/2004december/a4.shtml

United States General Accounting Office. (1981). *Cooperative Extension Service's mission and federal role need Congressional clarification.* CED-81–119. Washington, DC.

United Way of America. (1996). *Measuring program outcomes: A practical approach.* Alexandria, VA: Author.

Vines, C. A., & Anderson, M. A. (Eds.). (1976). *Heritage horizons: Extension commitment to people.* Madison, WI: Journal of Extension.

W. K. Kellogg Foundation. (2004). *W. K. Kellogg Foundation logic model development guide.* Battle Creek, MI: Author.

Warner, P. D., & Christenson, J. A. (1984). *The Cooperative Extension Service: A national assessment.* Boulder, CO: Westview Press.

Wessel, T., & Wessel, M. (1982). *4-H: An American idea.* Chevy Chase, MD: National 4-H Council.

Wholey, J. (1979). *Evaluation: Promise and performance.* Washington, DC: Urban Institute Press.

ROGER A. RENNEKAMP is head of the Department of 4-H Youth Development Education at Oregon State University, and has also worked as a county Extension educator and state evaluation specialist.

MOLLY ENGLE is associate professor and Extension Service evaluation specialist at Oregon State University, and is a former president of the American Evaluation Association.

King, N. J., & Cooksy, L. J. (2008). Evaluating multilevel programs. In M. T. Braverman, M. Engle, M. E. Arnold, & R. A. Rennekamp (Eds.), *Program evaluation in a complex organizational system: Lessons from Cooperative Extension. New Directions for Evaluation,* 120, 27–39.

3

Evaluating Multilevel Programs

Nicelma J. King, Leslie J. Cooksy

Abstract

Multilevel programs—that is, programs with multiple levels of administration, funding, and implementation—present dynamic and challenging environments for the conduct and use of evaluation. The challenges include questions, priorities, audiences, and purposes that vary at each level. This chapter discusses the challenges as well as the opportunities for increasing the value of evaluation at the federal, state, and local levels. Five areas of information are used as a framework for the discussion: (1) Who came? (2) Who cares? (3) What was the intervention? (4) What changed, and what difference did it make? (5) How much did it cost? Using the Cooperative Extension System and other cases as illustrations, the authors describe the relative emphases given to these questions at the different levels, the motivations for those emphases, and the opportunities evaluators can take to make multilevel evaluations useful to audiences at all levels. © Wiley Periodicals, Inc.

Many programs operate with funding from multiple levels of government as well as from the private and nonprofit sectors. For example, K–12 education receives the majority of its funding and oversight from the states but is also supported by the federal government and often receives additional support from local governments and nonprofit entities such as foundations. Temporary Assistance for Needy Families (TANF)

is a block grant from the federal government that requires matching funds from the state, and may also receive support from local agencies. Similarly, Cooperative Extension receives federal, state, and local funding, with the relative percentages varying widely from state to state and sometimes from county to county.

The multiple levels of funding, program guidance, and oversight can produce challenges for development and implementation of evaluation plans. Without specific attention to the concerns and indicators that are most appropriate for specific levels, evaluations of multilevel programs can focus on outcomes that "miss the mark" for some critical program constituents (Patton, 2008). At a minimum, evaluation designs for multilevel programs should take the multiple constituencies of the programs into account, and they need to acknowledge that varying constituencies may have their own concerns, which may or may not be addressed by any single evaluation. In this chapter, we organize our discussion of evaluation of multilevel programs around five broad themes that relate to potential constituent concerns, and that might vary by level:

1. Who cares?
2. Who came?
3. What was the intervention?
4. What changed, and what difference did it make?
5. How much did the program cost (or earn)?

We use the Cooperative Extension System to illustrate some of the issues in evaluating multilevel programs. (Note that our use of *multilevel* refers to multiple levels of administration, funding, and implementation, rather than to multiple levels of data sources such as program participants nested within larger groups.) The chapter elaborates each of the five themes outlined here, describing its consequence for designing and implementing evaluation of multilevel programs, and it concludes by describing the contribution that evaluators can make to evaluation conduct and utilization by focusing specific attention on multiple levels of evaluation. As an overview of the discussion, Table 3.1 summarizes the five categories of questions that evaluations typically address and displays how stakeholder interest in each question may differ across the levels.

Who Cares? The Importance of Multiple Stakeholders in Multilevel Evaluations

Stake (2004) defines stakeholders as "all the people who have a stake in the program, certainly the beneficiaries and injured parties, but also those who suffer lost opportunity because something else was not carried out" (p. 195). Sometimes the stakeholder group is relatively small and well-defined, but in multilevel programs the definition of stakeholders becomes

NEW DIRECTIONS FOR EVALUATION • DOI: 10.1002/ev

Table 3.1. Evaluating Multilevel Programs: Primary Information Concerns at Each Program Level

Research Themes	Program Levels		
	Local	State	Federal
Who cares? (*relevant stakeholder groups*)	• Program staff • Local support groups, including private, nonprofit, public agencies • Participants • Public	• State-level program staff • State-level support groups (including private, nonprofit, public) • Public	• Federal agency or program staff • Congress • Office of Management and Budget • National stakeholder groups • Federal lobbyists • Public
Who came?	• Audience appropriate to program goals? • Number and diversity, by type of program • Reached entire audience?	• Audience appropriate to program goals? • Number and diversity, by locality • By type of program intervention	• Audience appropriate to program goals? • Number and diversity, by state • By type of program intervention
What was implemented?	• Fidelity to curriculum • Appropriateness of format • Responsiveness to needs of participants • Dosage (duration and intensity of service)	• Appropriate for program funding source • Range of program variation • Responsiveness to defined state-level needs	• Fidelity to plans and funding source • Range of program variation • Cross-state collaboration
What changed?	• Participant knowledge, skills, attitudes, behaviors (KSABs) • Service priorities • Variation in impact among program staff	• Participant KSABs • Program implemented equally? • Program priorities • Variation in impact across local offices	• Impact on problem (e.g., better quality of life, reduced pesticide use) • Program implemented equally? • Program priorities • Variation in impact across states, modes of intervention
How much did it cost?	• Staff required • By program service • Inputs required by activities • Funding amount and sources	• Staff required • By program • By impact achieved • Funding amount and sources	• Staff required • Per funding source • In relation to overall impact • Efficient use of resources

more complicated and nuanced. There is broad agreement in the evaluation literature that evaluators must be aware of the concerns and expectations of various groups of stakeholders in designing and conducting evaluations (Merriam, 1997; Patton, 2008; Stake, 2004). The goals and concerns of stakeholders must be considered in the evaluation design because the quality of the program may not be adequately assessed if their needs are not addressed. In addition, some stakeholders can mobilize considerable political support for (or opposition to) an evaluation that is not responsive to their concerns. Although the process of identifying stakeholders is more complex in multilevel programs, the number of stakeholders and the relationships among stakeholder groups makes understanding their needs more important (Mayeske & Lambur, 2001; Patton, 2008).

The broad diversity of stakeholders at the federal, regional, state, and local levels can be illustrated by examining the case of Extension. At the local level, Extension stakeholders include program participants, program staff, local agencies, funding entities, support groups, local government officials, and the public. At the state level, stakeholders include statewide support and commodity groups, personnel from state agencies and commissions, involved faculty and administrators from the land-grant university that administers Extension, and state legislators. At the federal level, stakeholders include national support and commodity groups, personnel from the U.S. Department of Agriculture (USDA), other federal agencies, members of national commissions or advisory groups, and members of Congress and their staff (Bennett, 1993; Thomas, 2000). In some instances, stakeholders from any level may share opinions and program perceptions with stakeholders at other levels—an increasingly common occurrence due to the influence of the Internet. Evaluators of multilevel programs face a daunting job when they attempt to involve stakeholders from all levels in discussions about the program, but these conversations have two important benefits: (1) they build the evaluators' knowledge and understanding of the program, as well as the views and values of stakeholders; and (2) they boost the credibility of the evaluation process itself (Mayeske & Lambur, 2001).

In some multilevel programs, input on evaluation plans may be built into the reviews of program plans. For example, program evaluation plans may be included in comprehensive program plans developed by local agencies. These plans are then reviewed at multiple levels; at each level, multiple stakeholder groups may be involved. For example, at the state level advisory groups, commodity organizations, volunteers, and research partners might review the proposed evaluation as part of the review of the overall program. If stakeholder input is not built into the plan review, the evaluator must take the lead in obtaining it.

Involving stakeholders from various levels in evaluation of multilevel programs can be addressed formally or informally. Formal approaches may include design and administration of interviews or survey instruments addressed to their concerns, whereas informal approaches use less structured forms of data and information collection. In either case, the involvement should be deliberate and directed to the sphere of interest of the particular stakeholder or group. This requires that the evaluator possess a high degree of background knowledge and information about the program being evaluated, or failing that, the evaluation design must be built in stages, allowing time and resources to collect appropriate information about stakeholder concerns at successive levels of the program after evaluation data are collected at each level. This task can be made simpler by using reputational sampling techniques, which ask stakeholders at each level of a program to identify stakeholders at other levels, and by frequent cross-checking with program staff and others who are knowledgeable about the program to help identify those who are most appropriate for inclusion. This level of checking and cross-checking for stakeholder identification may seem repetitive, but it can produce a more definitive list of stakeholders, and it helps to identify those stakeholders who are regarded as key opinion leaders about the program being evaluated. The evaluator is also responsible for checking with the evaluation clients (the entity or agency commissioning the evaluation) about their perceptions of the importance of stakeholders who have been identified. Following identification, the extent and nature of each stakeholder group's involvement in the evaluation must be negotiated.

Who Came? The Importance of Program Participants in Multilevel Evaluations

Multilevel programs, like other programs, are directed to particular audiences. K–12 education programs, for example, are directed to school-aged children. Extension programs are directed to various audiences, including youths, families, agricultural producers, volunteers, and others, depending on the type of program. Evaluators need to be aware of the target audience for the program, how many of the audience members were served, for how long, and at what intensity.

Information about the number of participants is usually of interest to all levels of the multilevel evaluation, but information about the cultural or ethnic background of the participants may be of most importance at the state or federal levels, which often initiate policies and programs to promote cultural inclusion. For example, at the federal level the Cooperative State Research, Education, and Extension Service (CSREES)[1] conducts civil rights audits of state Extension systems, resulting in recommendations for increasing inclusion of underrepresented groups in local and state Extension staff and program participants. Information about duration and intensity of contact may be of interest to any level of the program, but if a particular level (federal, state, or local) requires specific amounts of contact, that level may be especially interested in evaluation data that track such contact. For example, the Expanded Food and Nutrition Education

Program (EFNEP), an Extension program that is largely supported from the federal level, requires that precise information be collected about the duration of each contact with program participants. Consequently, the 2006 EFNEP National Impact Report indicates that the program reached 150,270 adults directly for a minimum of six hours, and it provides ethnic and racial breakdowns (CSREES, 2006). Evaluators must be aware of the importance that the evaluation client places on participant data in developing the evaluation plan.

What Was the Intervention?

All evaluations, whether multilevel or single-level, devote some attention to a detailed description of the program. This description, at its most basic level, should include the program's logic model, detailing how the program is expected to change the participants' knowledge, skills, attitudes, and behaviors (or KSABs) (Donaldson, 2007; Mayeske & Lambur, 2001; Alkin, 2004). The program description serves two purposes: first, it gives the audience for the evaluation a common set of background information about the program; and second, it specifies how the program is expected to intervene in the problem cycle (Mark, Henry, & Julnes, 2000). For example, an Extension program may consist of a series of workshops, hands-on demonstrations, or field visits, and the program designers may expect that the workshops would change the participants' knowledge (through increasing awareness and understanding), skills (through hands-on demonstrations of techniques), attitudes (by both educating and demonstrating that the problem is amenable to change), and behaviors (by applying the information they have received in their own lives).

At the local level, there may be only one intervention to describe, or several. The evaluation describes the implementation of the intervention, its fidelity to the overall program goals, how appropriate it was for the participants, and the knowledge base or curriculum used. The local-level description usually includes information about the length, duration, and intensity of the intervention. At a state or regional level, however, there may be multiple interventions, or varying ways in which a single intervention has been implemented. The evaluation usually describes the range of this variation, and why it was appropriate to the needs of participant and stakeholder groups from various areas in the state or region. For example, the California Department of Education evaluated the state's migrant education programs in 2006 and devoted special attention to variations among the programs as well as to the state's overall coordinating responsibility (CDE, 2006). The evaluation at this level may also reference any statewide or regional-level programs plans and describe how closely the various programs adhered to those plans, or supply reasons for any major departures from the plans. If program congruence is an important dimension to the evaluation audience, the evaluator should assess the congruence of the state-level program model with federal-level goals.

At the federal level, detailed descriptions of individual programs may not be used as much as general program descriptions or narratives that describe the scope of the program variation. A good example of this kind of description can be found in the federal evaluation of Head Start Family Child Care Demonstration projects (Faddis & Ahrens-Gary, 2000), which offers an overall description of the implementation of a range of projects. Alternatively, one or more local programs may be described in detail, similar to a case study (Stake, 2006) to illustrate this scope of program variation. Because of federal goals that encourage cross-state collaboration, any regional and multistate program delivery efforts might also be included in the evaluation report.

Another example of how local-level information is used at the federal level can be found in some of the performance indicators that agencies developed to respond to the Government Performance and Results Act of 1993 or GPRA (Pub. L. 103-62). GPRA required establishment of performance indicators and collection and reporting of data on those indicators in annual plans submitted to Congress. However, for agencies that fund programs that are implemented locally, these indicators may focus more on the performance of program activities in producing outputs than on achieving desired outcomes. For example, in the USDA's FY 2006 Annual Performance Report the indicator for the "key outcome" of "promote more healthful eating and physical activity across the nation" is "application and usage levels of nutrition guidance tools," as measured by "pieces of nutrition guidance distributed." This information is gathered at the local level and then aggregated for reporting at the federal level, where it serves an accountability purpose. (At the local level, such information may be used primarily for management purposes, ensuring that adequate supplies of program materials are maintained.)

What Changed, and What Difference Did It Make? Identifying Program Impact

Measurement of program impact can be made more complex by the multiple levels at which a program operates. Stakeholders at all levels of multilevel programs have an interest in identifying program impacts, but the specific interests may vary by level, and impact measures that are regarded as significant at one level may not be accepted as appropriate evidence at another. For example, an evaluation of a mathematics intervention in an elementary school might focus on the degree to which the intervention helped students develop learning goals for particular skills, because classroom teachers may regard acquisition of learning goals as a critical building block for skill development. At the district or state level, however, the evaluation might be expected to focus on the extent to which student performance on standardized tests improved after the intervention was implemented (Campoy, 2005; Skrla & Scheurich, 2004).

In the case of Extension, there is sometimes a danger of confusing measures of the *effectiveness* of the practice being taught with the degree to which the target audience *adopted* that practice as a result of the educational intervention. In other words, because of the difficulty in getting accurate measures of adoption behavior, there is sometimes a tendency to focus on *what* is being taught rather than *how effective* the teaching is in changing the behavior of participants. For example, some nutrition education program evaluations report on the value to the target audience of adopting particular dietary and lifestyle changes rather than the extent to which participants actually changed those behaviors. On the other hand, EFNEP has historically collected food behavior data from participants and has therefore been able to supply measures of behavior change.

Taking an example from agriculture, a local researcher may evaluate the effects of an integrated pest management (IPM) practice on the need for chemical inputs rather than the effectiveness of the educational program in getting the audience to adopt the practice. In contrast, state-level evaluations of IPM education programs may be able to use records that track sale or application of specific chemicals because of regulations requiring that licensed applicators notify government agencies. Assuming the evaluator also has information on the timing and intensity of the local educational intervention, it might be possible to cautiously attribute any observed changes to the IPM education program. Even if the evaluator at the local level has access to the same set of records, the impact of the educational program at the local level may not be discernible. However, an evaluator at the state or federal level has the advantage of being able to aggregate data from a number of jurisdictions and then develop trend lines that may be attributable in part to changes taught by Extension educational programs.

The focus on accountability at the federal level in past years is affecting evaluation demands at other levels. Although GPRA was intended to increase attention to the results of federal programs, some programs have not been able to present data on program impacts, opting instead to focus on program outputs. To put more teeth into GPRA, another federal effort to increase attention to program impact, the Program Assessment Rating Tool (PART), was initiated by the Office of Management and Budget in 2003 (Gilmour, 2006). Unlike GPRA, which gave the federal agencies some discretion in establishing performance indicators, PART rates programs on 25 preestablished criteria, including the ability to report results with accuracy and consistency. The results of these ratings are presented on the Web site ExpectMore.gov, where agencies are categorized as (1) effective, (2) moderately effective, (3) adequate, (4) ineffective, or (5) results not demonstrated. A program can be classified ineffective on the basis of a lack of evaluation. For example, the AmeriCorps National Community Civilian Corps is described as ineffective for three reasons: its cost, the absence of a comprehensive evaluation, and the lack of measurable performance indicators. The program's improvement plan identifies "completing a rigorous program evaluation" as one of the ways it is addressing its PART rating. PART guidance specifically holds up randomized controlled trials as the best design for demonstrating results (Office of Management and Budget, 2004). Although it is not clear yet, it seems likely that this standard will increase the number of impact evaluations using experimental and quasi-experimental designs conducted at lower levels of multilevel programs dependent on federal funding.

How Much Did the Program Cost (or Earn)?

Program cost is an essential piece of information, but unfortunately one that few evaluators are truly skilled at assessing (Persaud, 2007; Rossi, Lipsey, & Freeman, 2004; Weiss, 1998). For multilevel programs, with funding from numerous sources, it is important to be able to link specific activities to particular funding sources. This is primarily an accountability question because funding agencies often restrict how funds are used. For example, in K–12 education the federal government has long funded Title I to furnish supplemental educational services for disadvantaged students (Title I of ESEA, 1965). Accountability for these funds is tracked primarily in two ways: by ensuring that the services provided by Title I funding go to youths who fit into the target population, and by the requirement that school districts demonstrate that Title I funds are spent only for educational services that supplement the school district's basic level of effort for all students. Evaluations of Title I program services can then focus only on those supplemental activities funded by the program. Cost information collected only for accountability purposes reflects an underlying assumption that the program being supported provides a public good. Efficiency and due diligence are expected; cost-savings are not an important outcome of the program.

However, in some multilevel programs, inclusion of cost information in the evaluation may be more than a question of accountability. Program cost (or cost savings) can be one of the program objectives. For example, in the case of the National Evaluation of Welfare to Work strategies, which evaluated 11 welfare-to-work demonstration programs, the cost savings of the programs were an essential part of the evaluations, not simply a question of recordkeeping (Hamilton, 2002). These programs used a variety of strategies, ranging from increased support for education to sanctions for lack of participation in job search activities, in order to move welfare recipients from the welfare caseload into the labor market. In addition to questions about the relative effectiveness of the strategies and related impacts on children and family well-being, the evaluation also asked about the government's return on its financial investment (ROI) in the program. Comparing benefits to the estimated net costs, the evaluators assessed the overall ROI for these programs and also compared the cost-effectiveness of higher-cost and lower-cost programs (Hamilton, 2002). In this case, the evaluation did not report cost savings by funding source; instead, the variable included in the evaluation was cost per participant. These were demonstration programs, and thus the cost information was an important part of the policy decisions that would be informed by the evaluation (Rossi et al., 2004). The public good (encouraging employment) had been determined; the evaluation question was how to achieve the public good most efficiently and effectively. To answer that evaluation question, cost had to be included in the evaluation.

In the case of cost information, multilevel programs are not so different from single-level programs. A single-level program that receives funding from multiple sources will probably be required to track use of the funds from each source, just as multilevel programs usually do. Similarly, any single-level program that is intended to save money, and not just achieve outcomes with the money provided, is likely to be required by its funding source(s) to collect information on cost savings. In either single-level or multilevel programs, the organizations allocating the resources have a great stake in data on program costs. Although the issues of tracking funding sources and considering cost-effectiveness cut across single-level and multilevel programs, evaluators of multilevel programs are almost certain to encounter the complicating factor of multiple streams of funding, and they may have to address requests to disaggregate evaluative information on program processes and impact by source of funds.

Conclusions: Implications for Evaluating Multilevel Programs

As this discussion has indicated, evaluating multilevel programs can be challenging. Each level of the program has distinct stakeholders and varying uses for evaluative information. Program staff at the local level may be most interested in collecting information for program improvement and for meeting the needs of program participants and local interest groups, but those at the state and national levels may be more focused on data that can be used for accountability purposes. These two needs can clash when local staff feel they are expending too many of their scarce resources on information that serves the needs of higher levels but is not particularly useful for implementing the programs.

Paradoxically, although the priority given to different evaluation questions may differ with the level, the basic information needs of the various levels are often similar. The most obvious example of this can be found under the question "Who came?" Essentially, as the program moves from the local to the national level, the participation questions are mostly aggregations of the previous level. The difference is in the emphasis given this information. It is important to know who came to a program, but a local service provider might be even more interested in learning how participants from various demographic groups reacted to the program activity. In contrast, for the state and national levels the numbers and types of people who participated in activities are important indicators of the overall fairness and reach of the program, as well as of its importance to the intended audience. Similarly, information about the basics of program implementation, the activities and services delivered, and how it was expected that the programs would produce the desired changes in the audience are usually needed by all levels, but the emphasis at the local level might be much more on the details of program delivery, while at the national level there might be more interest in aggregation by type of program, basic descriptive data, or fidelity to program intent. The use of questions that over lap across levels, though with differing emphases and priorities, can generate a tension for the design of evaluations of multilevel programs.

Despite the various priorities and emphasis given to them, the five questions that frame this discussion present a starting point for addressing this tension. It is essential that evaluators identify the common interests of the various program levels, negotiate priorities, and coordinate the data collection efforts. For example, if Extension at the federal level is interested in the magnitude of a particular problem across a variety of Extension jurisdictions, decision makers at that level must work with state and local programs to ensure that common methods are used to identify the problem, the appropriate stakeholder groups, and the likely participants; that data are being collected on all the essential categories; and that no nonessential data collection is being mandated. At the same time, decision makers at the national level need to keep the priorities of the local Extension organizations in mind. If local political realities require a slightly different definition of stakeholder or participant groups, then the value of consistently collected data must be weighed against the value of the service itself. Communication and coordination are the only way to identify these trade-offs across levels.

Evaluating multilevel programs is challenging, but it also offers opportunities. By coordinating evaluation needs, some efficiencies in data collection may be identified. The fact that consistent reporting and program planning frameworks are in use nationally makes it possible to streamline some aspects of data collection for evaluation, even if variations in local needs make interpretation of the data somewhat different from location to location.

In addition, multilevel evaluations can capitalize on the potential to build multilevel support networks for the programs. If local program staff and participants are aware of the evaluation audiences and information needs at the state or national levels, the data requirements placed on the local offices may make more sense. In an ideal world, such coordination would result in a system in which the data collected at any level are useful to stakeholders at all levels. In any event, the local program staff and state and federal decision makers need to work together to develop strategies for making data collected at the local level useful to local staff, and not just as a way to get continued funding. One approach to helping local staff with evaluation demands is to build evaluation capacity. For example, several state Extension offices afford a variety of evaluation resources for local staff.

The structure of multilevel programs also offers the opportunity for creative evaluation design. For example, in many multilevel programs several locations may be pursuing the same goals but using their own interventions. Either through regional coordination or by post-hoc evaluation syntheses, comparisons might be made of the effectiveness of the intervention strategies for particular audiences and circumstances. Within regions or states, local program offices could coordinate to collect more credible data by organizing joint evaluations. One way to realize some of these opportunities is by educating stakeholders at a number of levels about how priorities and resources vary. The current expectations of evaluation audiences at each level could be changed, if necessary, to allow more flexibility at that level.

Multilevel programs present dynamic and challenging environments for conduct and use of evaluation. The challenges include questions, priorities, audiences, and purposes that vary with the level. As our discussion has indicated, the multilevel program environment requires clarity about the intended use of evaluation data at each level and the feasibility of producing evaluations that could be appropriately used for the stated purposes. Limited resources also increase the need for negotiation about the evaluation responsibilities at each level. The complexities multiply the chance of falling into the kind of evaluation pitfalls that can beset any evaluation, but they also offer the opportunity to develop a deep and broad understanding of an approach to improving societal conditions, and a chance to target resources to programs that are having the desired impact. The evaluator's task is to take on the challenges and leverage the opportunities to make evaluation of multilevel programs useful to audiences, program participants, and other stakeholders at every level.

Note

1. The 2008 Farm Bill passed by Congress calls for a reorganization of the U.S. Department of Agriculture's Cooperative State Research, Education, and Extension Service (CSREES), the agency that is Cooperative Extension's federal partner. As this issue goes to press, the plan calls for the new agency name to become the National Institute of Food and Agriculture, with the reorganization to be effective by October 2009.

References

Alkin, M. C. (Ed.). (2004). *Evaluation roots: Tracing theorists' views and influences.* Thousand Oaks, CA: Sage.
Bennett, C. F. (1993). Interdependence models. *Journal of Extension, 31*(2). Retrieved March 3, 2008, from http://www.joe.org/joe/1993summer/a8.html

California Department of Education. (2006). *Improving services for migrant students.* Sacramento, CA: Author.

Campoy, R. (2005). *Case study analysis in the classroom: Becoming a reflective teacher.* Thousand Oaks, CA: Sage.

Cooperative State Research, Education, and Extension Service. (2006). *EFNEP fact sheet.* Retrieved February 29, 2008, from http://www.csrees.usda.gov/nea/food/efnep/pdf/ 2006_impact.pdf

Donaldson, S. I. (2007). *Program theory-driven evaluation science: Strategies and applications.* Mahwah, NJ: Erlbaum.

Faddis, B. J., & Ahrens-Gary, P. (2000). *Evaluation of Head Start Family Child Care Demonstration: Final report.* Washington. DC: U.S. Department of Health and Human Services, Office of Planning, Research and Evaluation.

Gilmour, J. B. (2006). *Implementing OMB's Program Assessment Rating Tool (PART): Meeting the challenges of integrating budget and performance.* Washington, DC: IBM Center for the Business of Government.

Hamilton, G. (2002). *Moving people from welfare to work: Lessons from the national evaluation of welfare-to-work strategies [Summary].* Retrieved March 18, 2008, from http://www.mdrc.org/publications/52/summary.html

Mark, M. M., Henry, G. T., & Julnes, G. (2000). *Evaluation.* San Francisco: Jossey-Bass.

Mayeske, G. W., & Lambur, M. T. (2001). How to design better programs: A staff-centered stakeholder approach to program logic modeling. *Journal of Extension, 39*(3). Retrieved March 3, 2008, from http://www.joe.org/joe/2001june/tt2.html

Merriam, S. B. (1997). *Qualitative research and case study applications in education.* San Francisco: Jossey-Bass.

Office of Management and Budget. (2004). *Program evaluation: What constitutes strong evidence of a program's effectiveness?* Retrieved March 18, 2008, from http://www. whitehouse.gov/omb/part/2004_program_eval.pdf

Patton, M. Q. (2008). *Utilization-focused evaluation* (4th ed.). Thousand Oaks, CA: Sage.

Persaud, N. (2007, November). *A cost analysis checklist methodology for use in program evaluations.* Paper presented at the annual meeting of the American Evaluation Association, Baltimore, MD.

Rossi, P. H., Lipsey, M. W., & Freeman, H. E. (2004). *Evaluation: A systematic approach* (7th ed.). Thousand Oaks, CA: Sage.

Skrla, L., & Scheurich, J. J. (Eds.). (2004). *Educational equity and accountability: Paradigms, policies, and politics.* New York: Routledge/Falmer.

Stake, R. E. (2004). *Standards-based and responsive evaluation.* Thousand Oaks, CA: Sage.

Stake, R. E. (2006). *Multiple case study analysis.* New York: Guilford.

Thomas, C. (2000). Commentary: Politics, context, and integrity. *American Journal of Evaluation, 21*(2), 269–273.

Title I ESEA. (1965). Title I of the Elementary and Secondary Education Act of 1965, 20 U.S.C.A. 6301 et seq.

Weiss, C. H. (1998). *Evaluation* (2nd ed.). Upper Saddle River, NJ: Prentice-Hall.

NICELMA *("NICKI") J. KING is a Cooperative Extension specialist in the College of Agricultural and Environmental Sciences at the University of California, Davis.*

LESLIE J. COOKSY, *recently elected 2010 president of the American Evaluation Association, is an associate professor in the University of Delaware's School of Education and the Delaware Education Research and Development Center, where she is responsible for developing an interdisciplinary graduate evaluation program.*

Lambur, M. T. (2008). Organizational structures that support internal program evaluation. In M. T. Braverman, M. Engle, M. E. Arnold, & R. A. Rennekamp (Eds.), *Program evaluation in a complex organizational system: Lessons from Cooperative Extension. New Directions for Evaluation*, 120, 41–54.

Organizational Structures That Support Internal Program Evaluation

Michael T. Lambur

Abstract

This chapter explores how the structure of large complex organizations such as Cooperative Extension affects their ability to support internal evaluation of their programs and activities. Following a literature review of organizational structure and its relation to internal evaluation capacity, the chapter presents the results of interviews with 10 selected Extension evaluators. Four structures for evaluation in Extension organizations are identified: (1) a separate evaluation unit, (2) within an administrative unit, (3) within a program area, and (4) within an academic department or school. The interviews addressed the philosophy and approach to program evaluation, what evaluators do, the perceived effects of organizational structure on evaluation, and reflections on the optimal structure for program evaluation in Extension. Several conclusions are presented: the evaluation function should be associated with a high administrative level in the organization, locating the evaluation function in program units appears to be preferred, roles and responsibilities of internal evaluators need to be clearly specified, internal evaluators need to work closely with administration and management to carry out their roles effectively and to incorporate evaluation into organizational decision making, and internal evaluators often assume other roles beyond their primary role as evaluator. © Wiley Periodicals, Inc.

Ideally, form follows function. But form, or the structure of an organization, also affects how well it functions. This chapter explores how the structure of large, complex organizations such as Cooperative Extension affects their ability to support internal evaluation of their programs and activities. According to Robbins (1990), "Organizational structure defines how tasks are to be allocated, who reports to whom, and the formal coordinating mechanisms and interaction patterns that will be followed" (p. 5).

Structure is one component of an organization's overall design. Well-designed organizations have a clear mission and are structured in such a way as to focus energy toward achievement of that mission (Burton, DeSanctis, & Obel, 2006; Galbraith, 2002; Gates, 2005). Other elements of design include the strategies and processes that are used to determine the goals of the organization, the patterns of division of labor and interunit coordination, and the people who do the work (Cummings & Worley, 1993).

With respect to internal evaluation, Love (1983) acknowledges that "structural factors are crucial to internal evaluation because they influence both the flow and processing of information and the behavior of the organization" (p. 12). In a recent study of Cooperative Extension evaluation professionals, Guion, Boyd, and Rennekamp (2007) call for additional research on placement of evaluators within Extension organizations as well as their specific responsibilities as they relate to evaluation capacity and functions in the organization.

This chapter begins with a review of literature related to several structural factors associated specifically with program evaluation in organizations. In light of these structural factors, the results are presented of an exploratory study that was conducted of a purposeful sample of Extension evaluators to investigate some of these structural factors and their relationship to program evaluation in Extension organizations. Finally, conclusions and implications for evaluation structure are given for both Cooperative Extension and other organizations.

Structural Factors Associated With Program Evaluation in Organizations

The literature associated with organizational structure is diverse and wide-ranging. One area that broadly addresses this topic is building internal evaluation capacity. Love (1983) identified organizational structure as one of 10 variables that can affect the success of internal evaluation within an organization. The two main categories of structural factors that are addressed here are (1) the location or placement of the evaluation function within the hierarchy of an organization, including structure and reporting relationships; and (2) the functions of the evaluation unit and the roles of the evaluator.

Location or Placement of the Evaluation Function. Stufflebeam (2002) suggests that the evaluation unit should be located as a staff operation at a high level in the organization to help insulate the unit from inappropriate internal influences and enhance its influence on decision making. Love (1983) and others (Food and Agriculture Organization of the United Nations, 2003; McDonald, Rogers, & Kefford, 2003; Sonnichsen, 1987) suggest that the internal evaluation unit and its leader should report to the highest levels in the organization and that evaluation should receive vocal support from senior administrators. Majchrzak (1982) supports this by stating that:

> Administrative support is defined as commitment of the administration to the use of evaluative information in managerial decision making and planning. An organization with little administrative support for evaluation will tend not to use evaluation information for managerial decisions. An organization with a high degree of administrative support will integrate evaluation into the organization at the decision making level. (p. 308)

Chelimsky (1994) concurs by stating that "real support from the larger organization's top management [is a prerequisite] for finding the resources needed to do the evaluations in the first place" (p. 494). Associating the evaluation function with a high administrative level in the organization increases its credibility and elevates its importance in the mix of management functions.

In their exploration of the roles and responsibilities of Extension evaluators, Guion, Boyd, and Rennekamp (2007) found that of 41 survey respondents nationwide, 37% were located in a program development and evaluation unit, 24% in administration, 22% were in an academic department, and 17% in a program area group. They noted that additional research was needed to explore how placement of evaluators within Extension organizations and their specific responsibilities were related to evaluation capacity and perceptions of the evaluation function. In a related point on evaluation bias, Scriven (1975) addresses whether to locate internal evaluators in their own in-house unit or have them attached to other project or program units. His preference is the separate in-house unit, although he acknowledges that this may result in loss of access to data or help in data interpretation because the evaluator may be considered an outsider. He suggests a hybrid model where evaluators are placed in various program units, coordinated by an evaluation officer in a high-level administrative office who coordinates the evaluators via regular communications and meetings. Scriven also points out that evaluators who are part of the program staff may lose objectivity because of "social and economic bonds to the development staff, compounded by the cumulative effect of repeated acceptance (or rejection) of evaluative suggestions" (p. 24). He suggests hiring external evaluators, if possible, or systematically rotating evaluators among projects to avoid potential bias. Related to this, Patton (2008) suggests an internal-external combination, where external evaluators are hired to examine and pass judgment on the quality and accuracy of the internal evaluation.

Functions of the Evaluation Unit and Roles of the Evaluator. Love (1983) states that in industrial settings, evaluation units have a staff support function and are responsible for both diagnosing problems and correcting them. By contrast, in human service organizations evaluation units are often dissociated from any particular function and operate as separate entities. This imparts a sense of isolation and perceived exclusiveness; consequently, the evaluators do not work closely enough with organizational management in carrying out the evaluation function. Love also notes that the evaluation function should be linked to planning and management functions and that the role of the evaluator should be clearly defined as that of adviser or consultant to program managers. He insists that evaluators should sit on relevant planning and program committees. Love (1983) comments on the linkage between managers and evaluators:

> The authority and responsibility for evaluation should clearly rest with senior managers and program managers. Evaluators should serve in an advisory role with respect to both the technical and the behavioral aspects of evaluation. Evaluators should participate actively with program managers in the process of using evaluation information. (p. 14)

Chelimsky (2001) notes that the roles, responsibilities, and functions of the evaluation office should also be clarified. Patton (2008) reinforces this by indicating the importance of carefully defining the roles of the internal evaluator to include attention to use of evaluation results. Chelimsky also advises that evaluators be responsible for translating the policy questions into evaluable ones, but the policy questions should never originate with evaluators alone; the organization's management, program staff, and evaluators should all be represented in this process. Likewise, Clifford and Sherman (1983) suggest that to function as a decision support person, the internal evaluator must be a member of the management team:

> The evaluation specialist and the manager have the joint responsibility of determining what data are needed to answer the question that the manager asks. While the primary responsibility rests with the evaluation specialist, there is a great need for two-way communication between the manager and the evaluator in the early stages of the task. (p. 25)

Clifford and Sherman (1983) contend that an evaluator's role is to help management in decision making. Operating in such a role, evaluators frequently take on peripheral roles as planner, operations researcher, manager, organizational development consultant, management trainer and consultant, and data-processing or information specialist. Love (1991) supports this notion and offers a list of both successful and unsuccessful roles for internal evaluators (adapted and expanded by Patton, 2008). Successful roles include management consultant, decision support, management information resource, systems generalist, expert trouble shooter, advocate for or champion of evaluation use, and systematic planner. Unsuccessful roles include spy, hatchet carrier, fear-inspiring dragon, number cruncher, organizational conscience, organizational memory, and public relations officer. Chelimsky (1994) calls for the evaluator to be an "evaluation broker." In this role the evaluator works with top managers to persuade them of the value of evaluation and the contribution it can make to policy or program management. She sees this role as a natural one for the head of an evaluation unit.

Patton (2008) interviewed 10 internal evaluators to determine how they employed a utilization-focused approach in their evaluation work. He reported five themes that characterized their work:

1. Actively involving stakeholders within the organization can be difficult because evaluation is often perceived by both superiors and subordinates as the job of the evaluator. The internal evaluator is typically expected to *do* evaluations, not facilitate an evaluation process involving others. Internal evaluators who have had success involving others have had to work hard at finding special incentives to attract participation in the evaluation process.
2. Internal evaluators are often asked by superiors for public relations information rather than evaluation. One mechanism used by several internal evaluators to increase support for real evaluation rather than public relations is establishing an evaluation advisory committee, including influential people from outside the organization, to provide independent checks on the integrity of internal evaluations.
3. Internal evaluators get asked to do lots of little data-gathering and reporting tasks that are quite time-consuming but too minor to be considered meaningful evaluation. Such assignments can become so pervasive that it's difficult to have time for longer-term, more meaningful evaluation efforts.
4. Internal evaluators are often excluded from major decisions or so far removed from critical information networks that they don't know about new initiatives or developments in time to build in an evaluation perspective up front.
5. Getting evaluation used takes a lot of time and follow-through. (pp. 218–219)

Guion, Boyd, and Rennekamp (2007) found that three evaluation activities make up a majority of the work of Extension evaluation professionals: supplying technical assistance on a specific element of an evaluation, managing or conducting the evaluation, and serving as an evaluator on a team.

They also found that evaluators were most likely to enter into the program development process at the point of evaluation design, or to develop evaluation questions. They concluded that to improve evaluation efforts in Extension, evaluators must strategize how to become engaged with programmers earlier in the program development process.

Several key points can be taken away from this brief literature review on the organizational structure for program evaluation:

1. The evaluation function should be associated with a high administrative level in the organization.
2. Locating the evaluation function in a separate unit may be preferable, but there are advantages in locating the evaluation function within program units.
3. Roles and responsibilities of internal evaluators need to be clearly specified.
4. Internal evaluators need to be involved with and work closely with administration and management to carry out their roles effectively and incorporate evaluation into organizational decision making.
5. Internal evaluators often assume other roles beyond the primary role as evaluator.

Interviews on Organizational Structure With Extension Evaluators

To further explore the factors discussed in the preceding section and to extend the work of Guion, Boyd, and Rennekamp (2007), interviews were conducted with 10 selected Extension evaluators. Evaluators were purposefully selected on the basis of my knowledge of their experience in Extension evaluation and the location of the evaluation function in their Extension organizations. These evaluators represented 11 state Extension organizations from around the country (one responded about two Extension organizations in which she worked).

The questions were open-ended and asked respondents to identify their current position, the organizational structure for program evaluation within the Extension organization, the philosophy and approach to program evaluation within the organization, what they do as evaluators, their perceptions of the effects of organizational structure on evaluation, and what would be an ideal organizational structure for program evaluation in Extension.

Two limitations of the study should be noted as well. First, these interviews represent the views of a select set of state Extension organizations, so the results and conclusions cannot be generalized to the Extension system as a whole. Indeed, not all Extension organizations have individuals devoted specifically to evaluation or give coordinated evaluation support to their program personnel. Thus, the intent of the interviews was to gain insights into the potential organizational dynamics that may exist with different structures rather than draw systemwide conclusions. Second, the interviews reflect the perspectives of Extension evaluators. Nonevaluator perspectives about the characteristics of these organizational structures—that is, from administrators, field educators, or campus-based educators—would certainly be of value and can constitute a direction for follow-up investigations.

Organizational Structure and Positions. A summary of the evaluation structure, evaluation scope, and reporting lines of the interview respondents is presented in Table 4.1.

In the case of a separate evaluation unit, there are typically one or more evaluation specialists affiliated with that unit, and close ties exist between the unit and central administration. Some evaluators in these units have an appointment or affiliation with an academic unit in the university as well. In two of these organizations, some purposeful restructuring was done in the past several years to elevate the evaluation function (one was a promotion and the other was a move from an academic department into Extension administration).

In the program area structure, evaluators are embedded within Extension program areas: agriculture and natural resources, family and consumer sciences, 4-H youth development, and community resource development. These individuals report directly to a state program leader, who reports to the Extension director. In the academic department or school structure, the evaluation function was originally located in Extension administration and then relocated into academic units for various reasons. In this structure, the evaluators have formal appointments that include Extension but also teaching and research. In this structure, evaluation is farthest removed from Extension administration; reporting lines to Extension are more indirect, project-related, and informal.

Table 4.1. Evaluation Structure, Evaluation Scope, and Reporting Lines of Interview Respondents

Evaluation Structure	Evaluation Scope	Reporting Lines
Separate evaluation unit (3)	All program areas	Unit head to director of Extension (1) Unit head to associate director or dean (2)
Within an administrative group (3)	All program areas	Director of Extension (3)
Within a program area (2)	Program area	State program area leader who reports to the director of Extension (2)
Within an academic department or school (3)	All program areas	Department or school head (3)

Note. Numbers in parentheses refer to number of evaluator respondents for each category (10 individuals total, with one responding on behalf of two institutions).

Philosophy and Approach to Program Evaluation and What Evaluators Do. The philosophy and approach to program evaluation was relatively consistent across all organizational structures. Three themes emerged: evaluation capacity building, evaluation for accountability, and evaluation for program improvement.

Capacity building is about building individual and organizational skills and abilities in Extension educators (specialists and agents) to carry out evaluations. This was a strong theme across all the individual state Extension Services represented in the interviews. Because Extension organizations offer a vast array of programs at the county and state levels, and because they typically have limited resources for program evaluation—one or two people at most—capacity building is one solution for addressing the organizational need for program evaluation.

Evaluation for accountability focuses on documenting outcomes and impacts of programs primarily for external stakeholders, especially the federal government. Indeed, several respondents commented that the federal plan and report were extremely significant in driving their evaluation system. In addition, in several organizations, outcomes and impacts are part of faculty performance reviews, which results in elevated staff interest in this type of program evaluation.

Evaluation for program improvement is about conducting evaluation to enhance delivery and effectiveness of the program and is driven by the needs of program developers. It may include both formative and summative components and therefore is more comprehensive than evaluation for accountability. One key difference between accountability and program improvement is the driving force behind them. Accountability is typically driven by an external force, while program improvement is typically driven by an internal need.

What evaluators do is driven by the philosophy or approach to evaluation in the organization. Because there is typically only one evaluator (although several of the organizations did have more than one person working in evaluation) and a large array of programs and people doing them, much time is spent training others to conduct evaluations themselves—capacity building—for both accountability and program improvement. In fact, evaluation is typically included as a responsibility in field and campus-based faculty position descriptions. Evaluators also mentioned giving technical assistance (responding to specific evaluation questions), coaching, mentoring, working with and serving on program teams, and coordinating the federal and state plans of work. Evaluators often function as program developers, and several mentioned using and teaching logic modeling as a means to build capacity and improve program evaluations. Some of the program evaluators with teaching appointments taught credit courses in program evaluation, which are often taken by Extension educators pursuing an advanced degree. In several units where there was more than one evaluator, staff split responsibilities across program areas to divide the work load. In one case, all faculty in the unit had some responsibilities for program evaluation. Although the majority of the evaluators' time was spent doing training, technical assistance, and internal consulting, they also conducted some evaluations, though on a rather limited basis. In some cases, these were grant-funded projects and in other cases they were internal Extension projects or programs.

Perceived Effects of Organizational Structure on Evaluation. Administrative support for evaluation was mentioned frequently as an advantage by the evaluators in units or those attached to an administrative group. Being associated with administration was perceived to elevate the importance of evaluation and make it more visible and accountable within the organization. One evaluator indicated that it keeps them more focused on the needs of the organization, or as another evaluator said, "It keeps me close to the pulse of what's going on in the organization." In two cases, reorganizations were made specifically to elevate the evaluation function within the organization (described earlier). Finally, one evaluator pointed out that by not being in program areas, they were more neutral with respect to any bias introduced in conducting program evaluations in the various program areas.

There were also some perceived disadvantages of being closely aligned with administration. Several respondents indicated that the evaluations they conduct may be perceived as less credible and rigorous compared to evaluations conducted by someone within an academic unit. Some would suggest that potential outlets for publishing the findings of evaluation studies related to a specific field, such as refereed scholarly journals, demand more rigor than Extension evaluation reports prepared for internal or external stakeholders. In addition, if evaluation is situated in administration, it can be perceived as administrative work and not programmatic work. Several evaluators mentioned the tension that sometimes exists between field staff and Extension administration. One evaluator mentioned the negative "stigma" of being associated with administration. Activities perceived as administrative work are at best seen as taking time from programming, and at worst a waste of time. This carries over to expending resources (dollars and personnel) for evaluation. In essence, resources expended for evaluation are perceived as resources for administration, and not programming. Another perspective was that evaluation is more accountability-focused if it is housed in an administrative unit. This stems from the fact that administration typically deals with Extension's most significant stakeholder—the federal government—even though most Extension funding is provided by state government. Much effort is expended by Extension organizations on complying with the federal plan of work; it is often used as the "stick" to motivate Extension faculty to do evaluations for accountability.

Evaluators embedded in program units indicated that because they are closer to and more familiar with the programs, they can do a better job evaluating them. This allows them to become familiar with the "rhythms and cycles" of the program and when best to introduce and conduct evaluation. They also understand where pressures and information needs are coming from, and they can take this into consideration in developing evaluations for the programs or in training others to conduct them. Because they are dealing with fewer people and programs, they are also better able to build evaluation capacity within their program area educators. Like the evaluators in separate units, the program-based respondents noted that the primary disadvantage of this structure was the potential for being less objective and introducing bias into evaluations. They addressed this by acknowledging it and taking appropriate steps in evaluation design and implementation.

In the department structure, evaluators thought they could spend more time on the subject matter of evaluation and indeed become more specialized. These evaluators felt that program evaluation coming out of a department structure is more focused on program improvement than on accountability (which they perceived to be the focus when evaluation is in administration), and that evaluations were more rigorous for the same reasons. Finally, without the stigma associated with being considered administration, they felt that they could build better relationships with field and campus-based educators around evaluation.

Toward an Optimal Structure for Program Evaluation in Extension. Although there was no ideal structure in most evaluators' minds, embedding or locating program evaluators within program areas did receive significant support from respondents. Some cautioned that this structure requires mechanisms by which evaluators in various program units can communicate with each other regularly. It was also suggested that in this structure, some type of external advisory board would be advantageous to ensure objectivity. Another organizing structure would be to have program evaluators within a separate evaluation unit assigned to program areas. This configuration would allow the evaluators to focus specifically on program evaluation, rather than getting caught up doing nonevaluation program activities that might arise if the evaluator were located in a program area.

An additional structure that was suggested was to develop a center for program evaluation within the university affiliated with departments and Extension. Such a mechanism would bring faculty together from various entities to carry out evaluations for diverse audiences, including Extension. The interplay of various entities and individuals would likely facilitate a broader understanding of the challenges of real-world evaluation issues, such as those related to sampling and rigor.

Finally, several evaluators pointed out that it is hard to come up with one ideal structure for program evaluation in Extension because there are so many subtle institutional variations and relationships within Extension organizations across the country. Nonetheless, it appears the critical

NEW DIRECTIONS FOR EVALUATION • DOI: 10.1002/ev

variables that need to be in place for program evaluation to be successful are a core staff of people (perhaps three or four) devoted to program evaluation, clear connections and support from administration, and connection to an academic unit. As one evaluator put it, "It has more to do with how the organization perceives evaluation. The attitude of administration has more to do with program evaluation than structure."

Conclusions and Implications

To conclude, I return to the key points from the literature review in light of the information from the Extension evaluator interviews, and I try to draw some implications for the organizational structure for program evaluation in Extension and other organizations.

The Evaluation Function Should Be Associated With a High Administrative Level in the Organization. This was certainly supported in the Extension evaluator interviews. However, it appeared to be a two-edged sword. Support from administration was acknowledged as a definite advantage in elevating the importance of evaluation in the organization, regardless of where the function was situated. But the stigma of being associated with administration was also a hindrance in getting evaluation done in Extension. The suggestion to consider locating the program evaluation function in Extension program areas may help in mitigating this issue.

Program evaluation needs the support of top-level administration in any organization. The administration stigma phenomenon may or may not be a factor in other organizations. One strategy to address this is to reinforce the importance of program evaluation for the sake of program improvement. Through my personal experience, I learned it was far more effective to promote evaluation as a tool for improving programs than helping the organization meet demands for accountability. If program staff view themselves as primary stakeholders for evaluation results, they are more apt to become engaged in the process of conducting high-quality evaluations. Results of such evaluations can be used first for program improvement, and then for accountability purposes.

Although Each Potential Structure Has Merits, Locating the Evaluation Function in Program Units Appears to Be Most Preferred. Embedding the evaluation function in a program area was supported in the Extension evaluator interviews as the structure most identified as ideal. The advantages were being closer to and more familiar with the programs, being more familiar with the rhythms and cycles when evaluation activities might be embraced or resisted, developing a better understanding of the information needs of stakeholders, and dealing with fewer people and programs. The primary disadvantage was the potential of being less objective and introducing bias in evaluating programs.

This structure may be appropriate for other organizations, acknowledging the advantages and limitations noted earlier. Bias and objectivity are the main issues to address in this structure. Scriven (1975) suggests that the way to address this is to have the evaluators in the various units coordinated by an evaluation officer in a high-level administrative office who organizes and communicates with the evaluators regularly. This structure was also suggested in the Extension evaluator interviews.

As a former program evaluator in an evaluation unit attached to administration, I see great value in placing evaluators in program units and support this as the most effective structure for program evaluation in Extension organizations. This is essentially the Scriven (1975) hybrid model. It is unrealistic to expect one individual to lend evaluation support and technical assistance to all programs, given the number of programs within Cooperative Extension organizations.

If Cooperative Extension is indeed serious about the importance of program evaluation, it must invest in an appropriate organizational structure and strategy that has a high probability of success. In this structure, Extension would have an individual in a high-level administrative position working to coordinate efforts of program area evaluators to ensure maximum effectiveness and continuity. Additionally, the program area evaluators would need to interact with each other and regularly share their progress. For significant evaluation projects, it would be advisable to employ external evaluators to review these efforts to decrease bias and ensure objectivity, as suggested by Patton (2008).

Roles and Responsibilities of Internal Evaluators Need to Be Clearly Specified. Evaluators interviewed suggested that they operate rather autonomously with regard to how evaluations are conducted. Nonetheless, the climate for evaluation is influenced by administration. My experience suggests that Extension administrators do generally recognize the importance of program evaluation. However, they typically don't understand the enormity of the task or what it takes to measure "impact" of all the various programs in Extension—a call that all administrators rally to and recognize in general. As Chelimsky (1994) states, "One problem impeding the use of social science research is that not all top managers and policy makers in government or in the private sector understand *how* evaluation can improve public programs" (p. 495). Good intentions are noteworthy, but administrators must have a clear understanding of what they are asking their evaluators to do and how they are organizationally structured with personnel and resources to accomplish this task. This is essential for Extension and other organizations. Moving to a better organizational structure may help address this.

Internal Evaluators Need to Work Closely With Administration and Management to Effectively Carry Out Their Roles and Incorporate Evaluation Into Organizational Decision Making. This was supported in the Extension evaluator interviews. Extension evaluators in the administrative units reported that they worked closely with administration in determining evaluation needs and focus, especially related to accountability. Given the importance of administrative support for evaluation, it is extremely important for evaluators in other organizations to work closely with administration to set the organization's evaluation agenda and to carry it out.

Internal Evaluators Often Assume Other Roles Beyond Their Primary Role as Evaluator. This, too, was supported in the Extension evaluator interviews. Extension evaluators often functioned as program developers, using logic modeling as a means to build capacity and improve program evaluations. Extension evaluators also mentioned offering technical assistance (responding to specific evaluation questions), coaching, mentoring, working with and serving on program teams, and coordinating the federal and state plans of work. Extension evaluators served many roles to get the job done. This is applicable and good advice in other organizational settings as well.

References

Burton, R. M., DeSanctis, G., & Obel, B. (2006). *Organizational design: A step-by-step approach.* New York: Cambridge University Press.

Chelimsky, E. (1994). Making evaluation units effective. In J. S. Wholey, H. P. Hatry, & K. E. Newcomer (Eds.), *Handbook of practical program evaluation* (pp. 493–509). San Francisco: Jossey-Bass.

Chelimsky, E. (2001). What evaluation could do to support foundations: A framework with nine component parts. *American Journal of Evaluation, 22*(1), 13–28.

Clifford, D. L., & Sherman, P. (1983). Internal evaluation: Integrating program evaluation and management. In A. J. Love (Ed.), *Developing effective internal evaluation. New Directions for Program Evaluation, 20,* 23–45.

Cummings, T. G., & Worley, C. G. (1993). *Organization development and change.* Minneapolis: West.

Food and Agriculture Organization of the United Nations. (2003). *The independence and location of the evaluation service.* Retrieved July 2, 2007 from http://www.fao.org/docrep/meeting/006/Y8912e.htm

Galbraith, J. R. (2002). *Designing organizations: An executive guide to strategy, structure, and process.* San Francisco: Jossey-Bass.

Gates, S. M. (2005). Organizing for reorganizing. In R. Klitgaard & P. C. Light (Eds.), *High-performance government: Strategies, leadership, incentives* (pp. 139–159). Santa Monica, CA: Rand.

Guion, L., Boyd, H., & Rennekamp, R. (2007). An exploratory profile of Extension evaluation professionals. *Journal of Extension, 45*(4). Retrieved December 3, 2007, from http://www.joe.org/joe/2007august/a5p.shtml

Love, A. J. (1983). The organizational context and the development of internal evaluation. In A. J. Love (Ed.), *Developing effective internal evaluation. New Directions for Program Evaluation, 20,* 5–22.

Love, A. J. (1991). *Internal evaluation: Building organizations from within.* Thousand Oaks, CA: Sage.

Majchrzak, A. (1982). Organizational context of program evaluation in community mental health centers. *Evaluation and the Health Professions, 5*(3), 303–333.

McDonald, B., Rogers, P., & Kefford, B. (2003). Teaching people to fish? Building the evaluation capacity of public sector organizations. *Evaluation, 9*(1), 9–29.

Patton, M. Q. (2008). *Utilization-focused evaluation* (4th ed.). Thousand Oaks, CA: Sage.
Robbins, S. P. (1990). *Organization theory: Structure, design, and applications.* Upper Saddle River, NJ: Prentice Hall.
Scriven, M. (1975). *Evaluation bias and its control.* Berkeley: University of California. Retrieved July 2, 2007, from http://www.wmich.edu/evalctr/pubs/ops/ops04.html
Sonnichsen, R. C. (1987). An internal evaluator responds to Ernest House's views on internal evaluation. *American Journal of Evaluation, 8*(4), 34–36.
Stufflebeam, D. L. (2002). *Institutionalizing evaluation checklist.* Retrieved February 21, 2007 from http://www.wmich.edu/evalctr/checklists/institutionalizingeval.htm

MICHAEL T. LAMBUR *is the evaluation and research leader for the National eXtension Initiative and a research professor in the Department of Agricultural and Extension Education at Virginia Tech.*

Taylor-Powell, E., & Boyd, H. H. (2008). Evaluation capacity building in complex organizations. In M. T. Braverman, M. Engle, M. E. Arnold, & R. A. Rennekamp (Eds.), *Program
evaluation in a complex organizational system: Lessons from Cooperative Extension.*
New Directions for Evaluation, 120, 55–69.

Evaluation Capacity Building in Complex Organizations

Ellen Taylor-Powell, Heather H. Boyd

Abstract

*Evaluation capacity building, or ECB, is an area of great interest within the
field of evaluation as well as in Extension evaluation. Internal Extension evaluators have long offered training and technical assistance to help Extension
educators conduct evaluation. Today ECB in Extension encompasses myriad
activities and processes to advance evaluation practice and evaluative thinking. They can be described in a three-component framework: professional
development, resources and supports, and organizational environment. This
chapter describes the Extension experience, highlighting practices and challenges
within each component, and presents the case of logic model dissemination as
an illustration. The authors discuss the distinction between evaluator and ECB
practitioner and call for clarity in purpose, role delineation, and expectations.
They include a simple logic model for evaluating ECB, which focuses on linking ECB investments to individual, team, program, and organizational change.
The authors conclude with a list of their own learnings and reflections as they
have faced the challenges and many rewards of building evaluation capacity in
complex organizations.* © Wiley Periodicals, Inc.

Evaluation capacity building (ECB) has emerged as an area of great interest as governments, organizations, and programs seek to enhance their effectiveness and accountability. Its goal is defined as strengthening and sustaining an organization's capacity to (1) design, implement, and manage effective evaluation projects; (2) access, build, and use evaluative knowledge and skills; (3) cultivate a spirit of continuous organizational learning, improvement, and accountability; and (4) create awareness and support for program evaluation and self-evaluation as a performance improvement strategy (King & Volkov, 2005; King, 2007).

In this chapter, we add to understanding of ECB by describing the Extension experience. We highlight the issue of role clarification and frame ECB within a three-component framework drawing lessons pertinent to other complex organizations. We start from the Compton, Baizerman, and Stockdill (2002) working definition of ECB as "the intentional work to continuously create and sustain overall organizational processes that make quality evaluation and its uses routine" (p. 14). However, we recognize and value the complexity of ECB and the force of context on its meaning and practice (Patton, 2007; Taut, 2007). ECB in Extension may or may not be part of "doing an evaluation." It may involve developing general awareness, skills, resources, and infrastructures to support evaluation, that is, the organizational processes that embed evaluative inquiry into the organization. Further, levels of intentionality may vary as well (Cousins, Goh, Clark, & Lee, 2004; Patton, 2007).

External and Internal Pressures for ECB

Three central pressures set the stage for ECB in Extension. First and most important is the external demand for accountability and documented evidence of impact faced by all federally funded organizations since the 1993 Government Performance and Results Act (GPRA). Extension is also funded by state and local tax money, as well as grants and contracts, so there are a multitude of stakeholders who want evidence of results. To meet these requirements, some Extension organizations contract out their program evaluation needs. Others choose the ECB route with self-evaluation as a way to manage limited resources.

The second pressure is internal. Extension organizations that desire to be learning organizations see evaluation as a core function (e.g., Cousins et al., 2004; Preskill & Torres, 1999). These organizations want to use and develop the intellectual capital of staff and promote critical inquiry and ethical conduct. In this environment, evaluation is not a separate or voluntary undertaking but is an organizational responsibility—a part of everyone's job. Extension educators are expected to participate in, if not conduct, evaluations of their programs as responsible public servants and to use their learning to improve program and organizational performance.

NEW DIRECTIONS FOR EVALUATION • DOI: 10.1002/ev

The third pressure relates to evidence-based practice and, in the university context, the culture of scholarship. University-based Extension educators are intrinsically motivated to check their work, link theory to practice, and use evaluation research to identify and develop best practice as well as document and communicate results. Conducting evaluation gives Extension professionals the means to present their work and gain recognition. Likewise, successful faculty promotion and tenure require evaluative inquiry that is valued by peers and external reviewers.

ECB Role Delineation

Organizational contexts and cultures vary, resulting in differing expectations for the ECB practitioner. Contextual features that influence the ECB role in Extension include how positions are funded, who has been hired (or appointed) as the evaluator, disposition of the evaluator, history of evaluation in the organization, organizational readiness for evaluation, and the location and ownership of the evaluation function within the organization, particularly the distributed nature of the evaluation role. Furthermore, ECB and evaluation are similar but distinct, a point clarified by Compton et al. (2002) but not widely understood among Extension evaluation stakeholders. A program evaluator is a professional who demonstrates skills and practices connected to planning and implementing an evaluation, while an ECB professional supports the processes and practices that sustain evaluation. As internal evaluators, often titled evaluation specialists, it is easy for these roles to be confused. Also, the ECB role is seldom the only responsibility of Extension evaluation professionals. Most have additional responsibilities: (1) federal reporting; (2) administrative tasks, such as civil rights reviews; (3) committee and policy decision-making assignments; (4) academic teaching or research; and (5) external evaluations or technical assistance. In a study of Extension evaluation professionals (Guion, Boyd, & Rennekamp, 2007), 42 respondents to an online survey described their roles as including these tasks: (1) offer technical expertise and assistance (72%), (2) manage or conduct evaluation (64%), (3) supervise, manage, or coordinate evaluation efforts (46%), (4) act as an evaluator on a team (44%), (4) coach or mentor (41%), (5) teach noncredit courses (23%), (6) perform institutional research (15%), and (7) teach for-credit courses (13%).

Negotiating and managing the ECB role in a demanding, often resource-poor environment where accountability and reporting dominate requires relationship building, as well as stewardship and vision. It involves negotiation and communication skills with a consistent focus on purpose and role. It can be a constant challenge to be seen as an ECB practitioner—building skills, processes, and infrastructures—rather than a program evaluator "doing evaluations," especially when performing the tasks of program evaluation is the key to securing buy-in and moving individuals and groups into the next level of capacity.

NEW DIRECTIONS FOR EVALUATION • DOI: 10.1002/ev

ECB Practice in a Complex Organization

Though there are commonalities, the Extension organization and the evaluation function differ across the states. Even program areas within a state Extension organization may have distinct cultures, philosophies, and support for evaluation. In this context, ECB relies on flexibility and the ability to seize opportunities.

Drawing on the work of others (King & Volkov, 2005; Milstein & Cotton, 2000), we use a three-component framework to describe ECB in the complex Extension organization, highlighting particular elements within each component (see Table 5.1). At any point in time, state Extension organizations may engage in any or all of these components depending on priorities and resources. The emphasis on each component varies, as do the activities undertaken.

Professional Development. Building knowledge, beliefs, and skills of individuals in evaluation is the most common and widespread aspect of ECB across Extension. In fact, ECB is often viewed as professional development (Duttweiler, Elliott, & O'Neill, 2001). Extension professionals work at different organizational levels and content areas, across geographic areas, and with various motivations and level of training. Few have a background in evaluation, though many have an advanced degree and may have completed courses in research methods. They come with their own epistemological and methodological interests. Further, they come with a range of orientations to evaluation: doubter, proctor, practitioner, consultant, scholar

Table 5.1. An Evaluation Capacity Building Framework

Component	Elements
Professional development	• Training • Technical assistance • Collaborative evaluation projects • Mentoring and coaching • Communities of practice
Resources and supports	• Evaluation and ECB expertise • Evaluation materials • Evaluation champions • Organizational assets • Financing • Technology • Time
Organizational environment	• Leadership • Demand • Incentives • Structures • Policies and procedures

(Douglah, Boyd, & Gundermann, 2003). Where Extension organizations have moved to team-based programming, expected professional development outcomes include the team's ability to conduct and use evaluation as a group—not just changes in individual knowledge, skills, attitudes, and behaviors.

Given the diversity of the workforce, a menu of professional development opportunities is often available within the organization—the exact mix customized to meet learner needs as negotiated by ECB practitioners, key administrators, and participants themselves. A continuing challenge concerns provision of appropriate professional development activities to meet the broad range of individuals with differing and changing needs, orientations, and evaluative responsibilities.

Training. Training continues to be a mainstay of professional development in most Extension organizations. Its purpose is typically to enhance knowledge, skills, and confidence so that participants are able to conduct adequate evaluations of their own programs. Customized and higher-level offerings relevant to a specific program or need provide more in-depth learning. Various Extension organizations offer online self-instruction modules and graduate-level courses for their faculty and staff, as well as for personnel from other organizations with fewer resources. Staff may be encouraged to attend regional and national evaluation conferences, workshops, and institutes.

Technical Assistance. Technical assistance involves personalized real-time consultation (Engle & Arnold, 2002) conducted face-to-face, by phone, via Web-based technologies, or by e-mail. These requests offer teachable moments and opportunities to build relationships, as well as possibilities for continued learning when the learner perceives the assistance as relevant and practical.

Collaborative Evaluation Projects. In maximizing team-based approaches and learning through practice, collaborative evaluation projects achieve greater impact and sustained change (Arnold, 2006; Marczak, 2002). Through collaborative inquiry, the team designs and implements an evaluation, gaining access to expertise and resources in a peer-learning, non-threatening environment that is grounded in real contexts and authentic activities consistent with social constructivist learning theory (Preskill, Zuckerman, & Matthews, 2003). Program and evaluation learning are best integrated into practice when the learning objective is clear and understood by all, and when the process includes time for reflection (Calvert & Taylor-Powell, 2007). Other forms of collaborative projects are developing evaluation materials and papers for publication, conducting joint presentations, and cofacilitating workshops and training sessions. The ECB initiative benefits from creation of resources and partnerships, while the participating staff member(s), including the ECB practitioner, gain knowledge and skills.

Mentoring and Coaching. Mentoring takes many forms. In one, the evaluation professional works closely with an interested colleague or colleagues over time, building individual knowledge, skill, and confidence. In another, she may serve as a coaching member of a program team, bringing evaluation learning to both the program and the coaching teams. In more mature phases of ECB, committed staff members become mentors for their colleagues.

Communities of Practice. Extension educators typically group by common interest for mutual support and learning. Intentional, formal evaluation-focused "communities of practice" are emerging as faculty and staff identify a mutual interest and organize themselves to learn from each other. They may form around a common problem, in response to a request, to share assets, or for personal growth. Members in these self-organizing groups recognize and value the commitment to shared learning and shared practice.

Extension evaluators have long supplied evaluation training and technical assistance. A more recent shift is a broadening of professional development to include a mix of activities and ongoing support to reinforce learning, consolidate knowledge into practice, and build capacity incrementally. The Oregon 4-H Youth Development program, for example, has systematized a four-part framework for evaluation capacity building that includes logic model training, one-on-one consultations on real projects, small-team collaborative projects, and staff involvement in large-scale multisite evaluations (Arnold, 2006).

Resources and Supports. The second component within the ECB framework concerns the resources and supports needed to sustain evaluation.

Evaluation and ECB Expertise. The strongest evaluation presence and sustained function are found in states that have invested in full-time evaluation positions. Few states, however, have more than one person employed full-time, and many are not formally trained in evaluation (Guion et al., 2007). Furthermore, *evaluation* and *evaluation capacity building* involve different competencies and strengths. To meet their professional needs, Extension evaluators have created and participate in an active Topical Interest Group of the American Evaluation Association (the Extension Education Evaluation TIG), which has a listserv for sharing information and materials. In addition, Extension evaluators connect with local, regional, and national Extension networks and workgroups; share expertise and materials; hire consultants; and access resources inside and outside Extension.

Evaluation Materials. Responding to learner demand for "examples that relate to *my* situation," Extension evaluators over the years have created a wealth of practical, Extension-relevant evaluation materials. Available in print and electronic formats, these materials support professional development activities, facilitate self-learning, and afford guidance for organizational ECB. They include topical booklets and how-to guides, PowerPoint presentations, tip sheets, case studies, worksheets, training manuals, and modules.

Evaluation Champions. Champions within administration, as well as scattered throughout the organization, are vital to ECB success. They must be continuously identified and nurtured to grow the evaluation culture and to withstand potential setbacks when a key ally moves or retires or when less interested administrators take the helm. Identifying these champions happens in various ways. Some champions are assigned by administrators to collaborative projects or evaluation responsibilities because they have influence with their peers, particular skills or interests, or learning or scholarship needs. Other champions self-select. We have found that working with these individuals over time, cementing relationships, and encouraging reflective practice help to build a cadre of key advocates that can communicate the value of evaluation and share ECB responsibilities.

Organizational Assets. To gain resources and guard against compartmentalizing evaluation, Extension evaluators build relationships, partnerships, and networks internally and across the university system. Tapping into existing assets offers expertise, infrastructure, and graduate student assistance that may not otherwise be available, as well as community field work opportunities for researchers and academicians.

Financing. Fiscal resources serve as both a signal and a tool of ECB (King & Volkov, 2005). Extension organizations use a number of sources of funds to support their evaluation activities, among them base funds, grant monies, and one-time financing. A common guideline offered by professional evaluators is to support evaluation of external grants at 10% of the project budget. This amount justifies evaluation allocations. States may designate a fixed annual amount to support a team evaluation project, or encourage evaluation as part of a program budget. But in general, adequate financing for evaluation remains a challenge.

Technology. A variety of technologies support the professional development activities of Extension ECB practitioners. In addition, many state Extension organizations and national networks have a significant Web presence with evaluation materials and online modules. One example is CYFERNet (http://www.cyfernet.org/), which offers program, evaluation, and technology assistance for children, youth, and family community-based programs. Many state organizations use survey software and electronic templates that facilitate state and federal reporting, as well as localized communications to reinforce evaluation's value to community educators and stakeholders. Sophisticated national systems exist or are under construction for collecting data and communicating results, with ECB processes supporting use of the systems. Technologies present untapped potential for learning about and from evaluation, as Hallie Preskill so vividly described in her 2007 AEA Presidential address (Preskill, 2008).

Time. "Not enough time for evaluation" is a frequent lament among Extension educators who juggle many competing priorities. Evaluation may be valued and supported by administrators, individuals, and the organization, but there are always other pressing priorities. Extension educators are service-oriented, serving communities by delivering programs in response to need. ECB facilitators walk the line between "quick" and "quality" to facilitate buy-in and align purpose with reality. Including evaluation-related time designations in job responsibilities, plans of work, contracts, and grants can help make evaluation expectations explicit.

Organizational Environment. A favorable organizational environment is the third component of the ECB framework, with these elements featured in the Extension experience.

Leadership. Where key leaders actively support and convey their support to others across the organization, ECB progress is evident. Extension has examples of such leaders who understand and express the purpose and value of ECB to others, set evaluation expectations, encourage, nudge, allocate resources, ask critical questions and request studies, use evaluation results and tell how results are used, encourage inquiry and critique, verbalize their support for evaluation informally and formally, and reward and applaud. In effect, these leaders share responsibilities for ECB and find ways to integrate evaluation into organizational life.

Demand. Demonstrable accountability largely fuels and legitimizes ECB and is helping to institutionalize evaluation across Extension. Yet vigilance is needed to ensure that accountability supports the ECB purpose (King & Volkov, 2005). In Extension, evaluation is often equated with reporting. We "tell our story" and write "success stories" to demonstrate accountability and promote programs. Evaluation as critical inquiry and learning may be subjugated to *doing* evaluation to satisfy funders or promote programs, with consequences for evaluation design and learning. For example, where county boards fund and support the Extension office and are content with reports that describe activities and the number of people served, staff are less motivated to ask critical questions or engage in higher-level evaluation. We also find that increased internal demand for evaluation and for evaluation capacity building, as noted by King (2002), can easily exceed organizational resources and capabilities. Educators in many Extension organizations are requesting more resources and assistance than strapped budgets and single evaluation professionals can give.

Incentives. Where evaluation is required in staff performance and tenure systems, we find motivation to engage in evaluation. The extent to which it becomes intrinsic depends on the individual, past experience with evaluation, and the perceived value of the evaluation experience. For some, evaluation becomes part of routine work. For others, once the tenure packet is finished so is evaluation, until the next external requirement appears, even though evaluation learning may have occurred through process use (see, for example, Cousins, 2007; Patton, 2008). Overall, we find the motivators that best embed evaluative inquiry to be the intangible incentives that come through leadership opportunities, recognition by peers, opportunities to demonstrate scholarship and grow professionally, having data to legitimize and validate one's work, and having information to improve programs and practice. In a survey of community-based educators in Wisconsin, 70% reported they engage in evaluation "to learn ways to improve programs" (Douglah et al., 2003). An additional incentive is the Extension educator's service orientation. The growing demand from community partners for evaluation training and assistance motivates Extension educators to increase their own evaluation expertise in order to teach others and respond to local needs. Using such motivators to guide and promote capacity building activities helps people engage.

Structures. Three structural features appear particularly relevant in the Extension case. First, successful ECB depends on communication structures that facilitate horizontal and vertical information flows across the entire organization. By increasing the use of electronic technologies and investments at the local level, we make this possible. Second, the team program structure, organized around issues, helps break down silos and facilitates collective action, collaborative inquiry, group problem solving, and synthesis. Additional peer-support and learning structures, such as program area liaison structures, evaluation advisory groups, and mentoring structures, can build on existing mechanisms to facilitate ECB. Third, data management systems are necessary to facilitate creation, management, and use of data, and can incorporate question banks for customized data collection, Web-based data processing, templates for using and communicating data, and processes for monitoring data quality and sharing lessons learned.

Policies and Procedures. A variety of explicit and implicit rules and procedures guide evaluation decisions and actions. Evaluation may be written into job descriptions and annual performance reviews. Likewise, we see evaluation policy in guidelines for tenure and promotion, scholarship, grants and contract proposals, internal grant awards, and expectations of program teams and organizational workgroups (for example, "create a team plan of work" or "develop a system to evaluate and communicate workgroup activities"). However, the nature, level, and expectations of evaluation may not be specified, and program areas or units may define their own expectations. Expecting evaluation without more formal written policy guidelines may result in evaluation becoming equated with end-of-session questionnaires, whose use can limit learning about evaluation options and approaches (Boyd, 2006). Policies related to financial resources or allocations for evaluation seldom exist.

Example of ECB: Logic Model Diffusion

A case example illustrates the interplay of professional development, resources, and support within the organizational environment in diffusion of the logic model at the University of Wisconsin–Cooperative Extension.

Background. In early 1994, a series of regional training workshops were conducted across the nation by the USDA's Planning and Accountability Unit (within the Cooperative State Research, Education, and Extension Service) to disseminate GPRA expectations and begin preparing states to accommodate the performance information mandates. The training included the new *input-output-outcome* terminology and a simple logic model to help states link program investments to results that paired up well with the widely used Extension evaluation framework, Claude Bennett's Hierarchy of Evidence (Bennett, 1975, 1979).

Process. The ECB action in Wisconsin started with developing practical, Extension-specific resource materials blending the new terminology and expectations with familiar concepts and processes to use in training and orientation of staff, starting with administrative leadership. University of Wisconsin–Cooperative Extension had a strong history of evaluation with longstanding funded positions and a newly hired evaluation specialist with experience using logic models. The associate dean and director, who actually enjoyed evaluation, served as a powerful champion and leader. She saw the logic model as a foundational framework that could bring cohesion to the fragmented program planning, reporting, and performance appraisal systems. The simple *input-output-outcome* graphic was transformed from an evaluation framework into a comprehensive program development model (http://www.uwex.edu/ces/pdande) to guide UW–Cooperative Extension program planning, implementation, and evaluation. This *logic model framework* became the basis for a new Web-based planning and reporting system, for the renovated performance appraisal system, and for the institutionwide impact reporting system initiated by the University of Wisconsin–Extension vice-chancellor in 1997.

Policy guidelines stating that faculty and staff would use a logic model framework for planning and evaluation were incorporated into staff performance criteria. Program teams were required to complete a plan of work and submit annual, outcome-centered accomplishment reports following the logic model framework. Internal grant competitions required logic model language. Monies were allocated to program teams to support planning and evaluation. The logic model language, the focus on outcomes, and the linking of evaluation with program planning began to appear across the organization. Demand grew for additional resources and training. The logic model was coupled with a practical evaluation planning guide and other print and Web resources to provide a common professional development framework, cross-program collaboration, and initiation of newcomers to UW–Cooperative Extension program development and evaluation. These activities reflect King's (2007) notion of "purposeful socialization" with evaluation understood as "part of the organization's core operations, not an add-on or afterthought, but simply the way business is done" (p. 53).

To build leadership in evaluation across the national system, a Wisconsin team spearheaded a four-day workshop that ran annually from

NEW DIRECTIONS FOR EVALUATION • DOI: 10.1002/ev

1998 to 2000. The associate dean and director led and cofacilitated the professional development opportunity, drawing wide national participation. One morning was devoted to logic models, spinning off into additional trainings and logic model resources. At about the same time, a cross-state team decided to use the logic model framework for developing a national nutrition education reporting system (Medeiros et al., 2005). Financial resources were secured and the face-to-face logic model workshop was turned into a public-access online self-instruction module (Taylor-Powell, Jones, & Henert, 2002). Simultaneously, a variety of influential external forces were in play, notably the "outcomes movement" spurred by the United Way and performance-based budgeting among county governments.

Results. No one anticipated the interest and demand for logic model training that emerged across the country, the extensive use of the Web site, and the diffusion process that unfolded. Today, the logic model forms the basis of the federal planning and reporting system and is widely used and adapted by Extension organizations for program planning, evaluation, reporting, and grantwriting purposes. This case illustrates a series of factors, events, and opportunities that occurred simultaneously within the external and internal environments, which were acted on in an opportunistic, incremental way. Such may be the reality of governmental and complex organizational contexts suggesting an "opportunistic approach to evaluation capacity development" (Boyle, Lemaire, & Rist, 1999, p. 14).

Cognitive, affective, and behavioral changes observed within University of Wisconsin–Cooperative Extension at the individual, team, and organizational levels include:

1. Increased focus on a program's theory of change, its underlying assumptions and the differentiation between activities and outcomes
2. Increasingly reflective practice among staff concerning their programs and their evaluation practice, suggestive of Patton's (2008) learning to learn
3. Increased skills in the methods and techniques of evaluation
4. Rising number of educators teaching and mentoring others in logic models and evaluation, suggesting increased motivation and ownership of evaluation
5. More effective use of evaluation resources to focus on appropriate evaluation questions
6. Improved ability to talk about and aggregate results across sites, with understanding of when and where aggregation is desirable
7. Improved communications with stakeholders about the results and value of Extension's programs
8. Increased ability to fulfill grant requirements
9. Increased number of evaluations undertaken

10. A common language, shared understandings, and a program development framework embedded in the organization, making evaluation a part of organizational life

Evaluating Evaluation Capacity Building

ECB is a process, and as such process evaluation helps determine its direction. Purposeful socialization and active facilitation of evaluation processes (King, 2007) have featured prominently in the self-reflective work of Extension evaluators. Much of the current evaluation effort of ECB within Extension focuses on process evaluation for directing and improving ECB, as well as outcome evaluation for measuring individual change and personal growth. Less attention has been paid to the expected collective benefit for the work group, program, or Extension organization. A theory of change, or logic model, for ECB may help an organization specify intended levels of achievement and make ECB expectations and roles clear. Outcomes may be defined relative to individual, work group, program, and/or organizational change and be linked to evaluation's ultimate goal of helping organizations contribute to social betterment (Mark, Henry, & Julnes, 2000). Figure 5.1 presents a preliminary, abbreviated logic model to illustrate levels and interactions of ECB outcomes and potential indicators of achievement.

As ECB matures, its higher-level outcomes demand attention and research. More rigorous and systematic evaluation is called for, relative to evaluation as an organizational learning and improvement system (Cousins et al., 2004). Approaches and models of ECB are developing in numerous contexts that warrant explanation and understanding—for example, differences related to depth and breadth of the ECB initiative, ECB connected to "conducting an evaluation" versus broader evaluative inquiry, and intentional versus more opportunistic approaches to ECB.

Conclusions: Observations Along the Way(s)

In continuously changing organizational contexts, ECB work is challenging and rewarding. We conclude with our own observations, which may be applicable to others working in similar organizations with multiple levels and complex dynamics.

1. Understand ECB as organizational development, not just professional development. Think about the individual, team, and organization simultaneously and maintain clarity in ECB purpose. We liken ECB to building a government monitoring and evaluation system as "a long haul effort, requiring patience and persistence" (Mackay, 2006, p. 9).
2. Use external demands for results as the lever, not the control. Calls for accountability can motivate an organization and its staff; use this

Figure 5.1. Logic Model for ECB Theory of Change

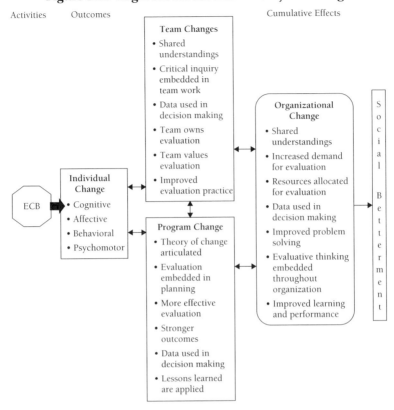

motivation to build the internal demand and intrinsic motivators that will sustain quality evaluation and build evaluative inquiry.

3. Practice evaluation through creative and mixed approaches. Opportunities abound for engaging staff and organizations to help develop "an evaluation habit of mind" (Katz, Sutherland, & Earl, 2002).

4. See every interaction as having educational potential. Use every opportunity, every teachable moment, and every serendipitous occasion to build evaluation capacity. This can include inserting comments in e-mails, engaging in hallway discussions, sharing articles and resources, and asking questions—approaches that are not necessarily planned or formal.

5. Not all staff need become expert evaluators. Consider diverse needs, experiences, and evaluative responsibilities. Work toward flexibility in designing and implementing the ECB initiative. Start where the learner (or the organization) is and build from there.

6. ECB practitioners tend to look more like evaluation educators and facilitators than like program evaluators—because they are. Being labeled a

program evaluator can be a challenge for the ECB practitioner if there is not broad-based understanding and support of ECB, or if staff members see critical inquiry and evaluation as the evaluator's responsibility instead of their own.

7. Identify and support those who care about evaluation. Never stop growing the pool. Encourage and support those interested in becoming evaluation leaders, mentors, and advocates.

8. ECB does not mean we must do it all ourselves. Engage partners, build networks and relationships, and access external expertise and resources to support ECB. Have fun learning along the way(s).

References

Arnold, M. E. (2006). Developing evaluation capacity in Extension 4-H field faculty: A framework for success. *American Journal of Evaluation, 27*(2), 257–269.

Bennett, C. (1975). Up the hierarchy. *Journal of Extension, 13*(2), 7–12.

Bennett, C. (1979). *Analyzing impacts of extension programs.* Washington, DC: U.S. Department of Agriculture, Science and Education Administration (ESC-575).

Boyd, H. (2006, November). *Internal evaluation and Extension education: Cultural competence within one organization.* Paper presented at the annual meeting of the American Evaluation Association, Portland, OR.

Boyle, R., Lemaire, D., & Rist, R. (1999). Introduction: Building evaluation capacity. In R. Boyle & D. Lemaire (Eds.), *Building effective evaluation capacity: Lessons from practice.* New Brunswick, NJ: Transaction.

Calvert, M., & Taylor-Powell, E. (2007, November). *Facilitating collaborative evaluation projects for building and sustaining evaluation capacity: Reflections and lessons learned.* Roundtable discussion presented at the annual meeting of the American Evaluation Association, Baltimore, MD.

Compton, D. W., Baizerman, M., & Stockdill, S. D. (Eds.). (2002). *The art, craft, and science of evaluation capacity building. New Directions for Evaluation, 93.*

Cousins, J. B. (Ed.). (2007). *Process use in theory, research, and practice. New Directions for Evaluation, 116.*

Cousins, B., Goh, S., Clark, S., & Lee, L. (2004). Integrating evaluation inquiry into the organizational culture: A review and synthesis of the knowledge base. *Canadian Journal of Program Evaluation, 2004, 19*(2), 99–141.

Douglah, M., Boyd, H., & Gundermann, D. (2003, November). *Nurturing the development of an evaluation culture in a public educational agency.* Paper presented at the annual meeting of the American Evaluation Association, Atlanta, GA.

Duttweiler, M., Elliott, E., & O'Neill, M. (2001, November). *Strategies for mainstreaming evaluation practice within local Cooperative Extension units.* Paper presented at the annual meeting of the American Evaluation Association, St. Louis, MO.

Engle, M., & Arnold, M. (2002). *When the student is ready: Capitalizing on an opportunity to teach evaluation.* Unpublished manuscript, Oregon State University, Corvallis.

Guion, L., Boyd, H., & Rennekamp, R. (2007). An exploratory profile of Extension evaluation professionals. *Journal of Extension, 45*(4). Retrieved February 10, 2008 from http://www.joe.org/joe/2007august/a5p.shtml

Katz, S., Sutherland, S., & Earl, L. (2002). Developing an evaluation habit of mind. *Canadian Journal of Program Evaluation, 17*(2), 103–119.

King, J. A. (2002). Building the evaluation capacity of a school district. In D. W. Compton, M. Baizerman, & S. H. Stockdill (Eds.), *The art, craft, and science of evaluation capacity building. New Directions for Evaluation, 93,* 63–80.

King, J. A. (2007). Developing evaluation capacity through process use. In J. B. Cousins (Ed.), *Process use in theory, research, and practice. New Directions for Evaluation, 116*, 45–59.

King, J. A., & Volkov, B. (2005). A framework for building evaluation capacity based on the experiences of three organizations. *CURA Reporter, 35*(3), 10–16.

Mackay, K. (2006). *Evaluation capacity development: Institutionalization of monitoring and evaluation systems to improve public sector management* (Operations Evaluation Department ECD Working Paper Series, 15, report number 37828). Washington, DC: World Bank.

Marczak, M. (2002, February). Capacity building and beyond: Evaluator's role in Extension. *Hear It from the Board.* Retrieved February 10, 2008 from http://danr.ucop.edu/eee-aea/AEA_HearItFromTheBoardFeb2002.pdf

Mark, M., Henry, G., & Julnes, G. (2000). *Evaluation: An integrated framework for understanding, guiding, and improving policies and programs.* San Francisco: Jossey-Bass.

Medeiros, L., Butkus, S., Chipman, H., Cox, R., Jones, L., & Little, D. (2005). A logic model framework for community nutrition education. *Journal of Nutrition Education and Behavior, 37*(4), 197–202.

Milstein, B., & Cotton, D. (2000, March 28). *Working draft: Defining concepts for the presidential strand on building evaluation capacity* [Msg 17390]. Message posted to American Evaluation Discussion List, http://bama.ua.edu/cgi-bin

Patton, M. Q. (2007). Process use as a usefulism. In J. B. Cousins (Ed.), *Process use in theory, research, and practice. New Directions for Evaluation, 116*, 99–112.

Patton, M. Q. (2008). *Utilization-focused evaluation* (4th ed.). Thousand Oaks, CA: Sage.

Preskill, H. (2008). Evaluation's second act: A spotlight on learning. *American Journal of Evaluation, 29*(2), 127–138.

Preskill, H., & Torres, R. (1999). *Evaluative inquiry for learning in organizations.* Thousand Oaks, CA: Sage.

Preskill, H., Zuckerman, B., & Matthews, B. (2003). An exploratory study of process use: Findings and implications for future research. *American Journal of Evaluation, 24*(4), 423–442.

Taut, S. (2007). Defining evaluation capacity building: Utility considerations. [Letter to the editor]. *American Journal of Evaluation, 28*(1), 120.

Taylor-Powell, E., Jones, L., & Henert, E. (2002). *Enhancing program performance with logic models.* University of Wisconsin–Extension. Retrieved February 10, 2008, from http://www1.uwex.edu/ces/lmcourse/

ELLEN TAYLOR-POWELL is an evaluation specialist at the University of Wisconsin–Cooperative Extension.

HEATHER H. BOYD is a program evaluation specialist with Virginia Cooperative Extension and was chair of the Extension Education Evaluation topical interest group of the American Evaluation Association.

Braverman, M. T., & Arnold, M. E. (2008). An evaluator's balancing act: Making decisions about methodological rigor. In M. T. Braverman, M. Engle, M. E. Arnold, & R. A. Rennekamp (Eds.), *Program evaluation in a complex organizational system: Lessons from Cooperative Extension. New Directions for Evaluation, 120,* 71–86.

6

An Evaluator's Balancing Act: Making Decisions About Methodological Rigor

Marc T. Braverman, Mary E. Arnold

Abstract

Methodological rigor consists of a series of elements that, in combination, determine the confidence with which conclusions can be drawn from the evaluation results. These elements include evaluation design, conceptualization of constructs, measurement strategies, time frames, program integrity, and others. The authors examine the factors that influence rigor-related evaluation planning decisions and the relationship of rigor to evaluation use by the sponsoring organization. Rather than following generalized predetermined standards, decisions about rigor should be based on the specific organizational context, information needs for the evaluation, and anticipated benefits and costs of available methodological alternatives. Extension offers a rich organizational context for discussion because of the diversity and complexity of its funding, stakeholders, programs, and evaluations. Several roles are proposed through which evaluators can promote organizational learning with regard to the contribution of methodological rigor to sound evaluation practice. Two Extension evaluations are presented as examples; though they reflect differing levels of rigor, both were thoughtfully planned and resulted in strong use of findings. © Wiley Periodicals, Inc.

NEW DIRECTIONS FOR EVALUATION, no. 120, Winter 2008 © Wiley Periodicals, Inc.
Published online in Wiley InterScience (www.interscience.wiley.com) • DOI: 10.1002/ev.277

The pressures for publicly funded programs to demonstrate account-ability have never been higher, as legislators and administrators call for documentation of effectiveness to support their resource alloca-tion decisions (Schweigert, 2006). Programs have a crucial stake in being able to make a convincing case for their potential value, and their existence often hinges on the availability of persuasive evaluation evidence. Attention to sound methodology maximizes the influence that an evaluation ulti-mately has in making that case and in developing an understanding of a program's value, impact, and underlying mechanisms.

Methodological rigor is a characteristic of evaluation studies that refers to the strength of the design's underlying logic and the confidence with which conclusions can be drawn. An evaluation that incorporates attention to methodological rigor will be in a better position to afford evidence and conclusions that can stand up to critical analysis. However, although rigor is valued as a hallmark of high-quality evaluations, it also carries a cost in terms of required resources and potential program disruptions to accom-modate the data collection process. Evaluators are acutely aware of the implications of various methodological decisions, and they frequently bear the primary responsibility of maximizing the rigor of an evaluation while accommodating resource limitations and the competing concerns of pro-gram stakeholders.

This chapter examines these issues in the context of evaluation practice within organizations. We discuss the components of methodological rigor and the factors that influence methodological choices in planning evalua-tions. We describe how these issues are reflective of particular organizational settings, and we examine the role that evaluators can play in ensuring rigor within their organization. Finally, we present some examples from the Coop-erative Extension system. Extension provides a rich context for illustrating this discussion because of its numerous audiences and diverse local program settings. In addition, because Extension's funding includes federal, state, and county government sources, questions about program effectiveness and pub-lic accountability are always at the forefront of Extension planning.

The Elements of Methodological Rigor

In our use of the term *methodological rigor,* we refer to a number of specific elements of a program evaluation such as the evaluation's design, concep-tualization of outcomes, and measurement strategies. Each element leads to a series of decisions about specific methodological details. Table 6.1 describes the elements and shows a sampling of the accompanying decisions for purposes of illustration. These components combine to produce the underlying logic in how the evaluation addresses the questions of interest.

Methodological decisions establish the nature of the data as well as the way those data are collected, analyzed, and interpreted. The decisions also have an impact on the various forms of bias—defined as systematic error

NEW DIRECTIONS FOR EVALUATION • DOI: 10.1002/ev

Table 6.1. The Elements of Methodological Rigor and Related Decisions About Evaluation Planning

Element	Description	Example Methodological Decisions
Evaluation design	• Determination of how, when, and from whom data will be collected • Structure of the critical comparisons that will address the questions of interest (Lipsey, 1993; Shadish, Cook, & Campbell, 2002)	• Should we use randomized control groups, intact comparison groups, or a single-group pretest-posttest design? • Should we use a single pretest or multiple pretests to discern the patterns that exist prior to the program?
Conceptualization of program constructs and outcomes	• Choices about which outcomes will be examined • Decisions about how outcomes will be translated into variables that accommodate monitoring and measurement (Bennett & Rockwell, 1996)	• Should we include long-term target behaviors (which require an extended measurement period) and/or shorter-term predictors such as intentions and attitudes (which can be measured at program's conclusion)? • Should we include physiological measures (e.g., weight, markers of heart disease) and/or behaviors that are known to be closely related to our target health outcomes (e.g., eating and exercise habits)?
Measurement strategies	Translation of the selected constructs and outcomes into measurement strategies and instruments, including: • Form of data—surveys, observations, biochemical measures, etc. • Selection or development of particular scales • Mode of respondent interaction: paper and pencil, telephone, in-person, e-mail, Web-based	• Will behavioral self-report be sufficient, or should it be supplemented with biochemical markers, behavioral observations, peer ratings, or other measurement strategies? • Should we administer our questionnaire through in-person administration, telephone interviews, or Web surveys? • Use a preexisting scale or develop our own? • Should we use one measure for our key variables or triangulate using several measurement approaches? • Should we hire outside data collectors who are independent of the program development team?
Time frame of the evaluation study	The time period designated for monitoring: • The program • The outcomes of interest (Rogers et al., 2000)	• Do we need measurement at both the program's immediate conclusion and at long-term follow-up? • For long-term follow-up, should we measure at 6 months, 1 year, or 2 years (or some combination)?

(Continued)

Table 6.1. Continued

Element	Description	Example Methodological Decisions
Program integrity	The conditions under which the program was actually delivered, including, e.g., • The fidelity of its implementation • Changes in the program environment over time • Variations across program sites (Dennis, 1994; St. Pierre, 2004)	• Should we obtain an objective record of program delivery for later coding and analysis, such as through videotape, audiotape, or other procedure? • At our program sites, how much variation in program delivery will we accept in determining how the program was delivered? • Will we plan for including or excluding program sites on the basis of some minimum degree of implementation fidelity? • What should our fidelity standards be?
Program participation and attrition	• Loss of participants from the program or the evaluation study • Inconsistency in program attendance • Other variations in program dosage	• Should we attempt to collect posttest measures on program dropouts? • How will they be treated in the data analysis? • How many of our (e.g.) ten program sessions must participants attend to be categorized as having fully participated? • Should our analysis take account of partial program participation? • What will be the parameters of partial participation? • What level of resources should we expend in persuading participants to remain in the evaluation study, if not in the program itself?
Statistical analyses	For evaluations that involve quantitative analyses: • Number and appropriateness of statistical tests • Statistical power considerations including adequate sample size, strong reliability of measures, and other factors (Lipsey, 1998)	• Is the number of statistical tests sufficiently limited to yield an acceptable overall alpha rate? • What is the statistical power of our analyses, given specified potential program effect sizes?

(Braverman, 1996)—that may be present in the data and the evaluator's ability to assess that bias. For example, use of several measures, rather than a single measure, to address a particular behavioral outcome can increase confidence that any potential measurement bias will be identified and assessed.

Methodological Consensus and Debate. Methodological rigor is directly related to the acceptability of evaluation evidence. For many of the elements of rigor, there may be general consensus among methodologists regarding what kinds of approaches are strongest, that is, which ones will result in a higher level of confidence in the findings. For an impact evaluation, for example, a design that gives a counterfactual estimate (that is, a no-treatment expectation) is stronger than a design that examines only change over time in the program's participants. Similarly, for programs designed to influence a particular behavior, evaluations are strongest if they include measures of the behavior in question rather than relying solely on its correlates or predictors. In other cases, however, there are disagreements about which options produce the best type of evidence. Experienced evaluators know that decisions on method often need to be perceived in shades of gray rather than black and white (Patton, 2008).

One example of this debate is the advisability of using randomized control group designs in comparative evaluations. Despite a widespread view that this is the gold standard for evaluating program impact—that is, the strongest, most convincing type of design—randomized designs tend to present characteristic problems and challenges (Chatterji, 2007; Chelimsky, 2007), which sometimes make other design options preferable. Thus evaluators sometimes overlook the degree of flexibility and creativity that can be applied to their decisions about methodology.

Factors That Drive Decisions About Methodological Rigor

To the extent that consensus may exist as to the strongest methodological approaches for an evaluation context, why wouldn't an evaluation team routinely plan for the most rigorous design possible to address a particular evaluation question? Several other factors play a role in influencing these decisions. First we consider three factors that can be characterized as costs.

Money. Evaluations are expensive, routinely requiring considerable monetary resources for the processes of planning, data collection, interpretation, and reporting. For a program evaluation lasting a year or more, a contract with an outside evaluator can easily cost $25,000, and often considerably more. Alternatively, assigning a team within the program or organization to conduct the evaluation—assuming the expertise is present—can tie up much organizational time in that task. Thus programs often determine the details of an evaluation on the basis of a finite amount of funding that is available for that purpose.

Time. The costs in time are conceptualized in several ways. Personnel time, of course, can be translated directly into monetary costs. In addition, time may be required from stakeholder advisory groups and other individuals who participate without monetary compensation, but for whom the evaluation team may be mindful to attempt to limit their commitment. Finally, there is calendar time: it may be methodologically advisable to measure participant characteristics and behaviors a year or more after a program ends, but for any number of reasons it might not be possible to wait that long. In such cases, the evaluation team has to consider the status of relevant outcome variables within the time horizon that is available. This may mean having to give program participants a posttest at the conclusion of the final program session, instead of attempting to track long-term changes in target behaviors.

Burden on Participants. In many respects the burden of a rigorous evaluation falls on the shoulders of the program clientele, their families, and the program staff. Many of the elements of methodological rigor require either increased control of program conditions or more information about program participants. These requirements translate into greater demands on program clientele and staff, and in some cases members of the program's larger target audiences who have no involvement with the program. Participants may find themselves being asked to complete longer questionnaires or interviews, participate in multiple measurement sessions instead of just one, be available for measurement at specific times, and supply extensive or sensitive information about themselves and their families. In addition, evaluations using comparison groups make these demands on individuals who know little or nothing about the program, in addition to individuals who have participated in it actively. Furthermore, in longitudinally oriented evaluations the evaluation team maintains contact with participants and requests that they take part in measurement activities for months or years after their program involvement has ended.

From the perspective of enhancing rigor, these distal measures (for example, of adolescents' substance use, pregnancy status, school success, and so on) will yield great benefits for developing an understanding of program impact and building buy-in for the strength of the evaluation study. However, one can understand the enthusiasm not being shared by the individual respondents who must submit to these demands. Evaluators who are not successful in communicating the rationale, impetus, and desirability for these requirements run the risk of high respondent attrition, as well as being perceived with some resentment as self-interested, "ivory tower" researchers.

When evaluation planners take into account these cost factors in their methodological decisions, they balance the relative gain against relative cost for every component of the plan. From a purely rational perspective, one would expect the evaluation team to consider stakeholder information needs and the anticipated uses of the evaluation, and choose the strongest methodological approaches within the constraints of those costs. However,

NEW DIRECTIONS FOR EVALUATION • DOI: 10.1002/ev

additional factors also come into play that are external to the logic of the evaluation's attempt to balance benefits and costs.

Funder Requirements. Program funders often explicitly spell out the components that must be present in the evaluation process. For example, in funding Extension's Expanded Food and Nutrition Education Program (EFNEP), the U.S. Department of Agriculture has identified an extensive set of questionnaire items for use in local program evaluations, including 10 required items and numerous others that can be added as appropriate to reflect local program content. By contrast, other funders, seeking to encourage evaluation of any kind, might simply issue broad evaluation requirements, leaving the major decisions to the funding recipients.

Opportunity. Some methodological options cannot be pursued because there is no opportunity to do so. We have already mentioned the limitations that may exist for the timeframe of an evaluation. Another example is the use of comparison or control groups. It may be that there are no groupings of a program's target audience outside of the program setting. This may be more of a challenge when dealing with community-based programs than with programs that are implemented within institutional settings such as schools, in which comparison groups can be more easily recruited. Furthermore, even if potential comparison groups are available (for example, in working with 4-H community clubs), there may not be an option to reassign group membership to create randomized control groups; thus there may exist a quasi-experimental design option while there is no randomization option.

Standards and Trends in the Field. Some professional societies issue sets of standards for evaluation studies. The Society for Prevention Research (2004), for example, convened a committee to develop a set of criteria by which to judge effectiveness claims for prevention programs, which was adopted by the board of directors and disseminated by the society. More generally, evaluation planning decisions may be reflective of work that is being conducted by colleagues, published in journals, and reported at professional conferences. For example, longtime Extension evaluators may remember a period in the 1980s when youth self-esteem was an outcome that attracted strong interest from program planners, and self-esteem scales were being almost routinely appended to the evaluations of 4-H youth development programs.

Requirements for Formal Program Recognition and Legitimation. Several federal and state agencies maintain registries of programs that they deem to be effective, on the basis of evaluation evidence that has been submitted by the programs and reviewed by advisory panels. Examples are the federal Department of Education's What Works Clearinghouse (Institute of Education Sciences, 2008) and the Substance Abuse and Mental Health Services Administration's (2008) National Registry of Evidence-based Programs and Practices. Frequently, these lists constitute the only acceptable program options for school districts or other recipients of the agency's funding—a phenomenon referred to by Weiss, Murphy-Graham, Petrosino, and Gandhi (2008) as "imposed use" of evaluation studies. Inclusion on these lists can be a powerful driver for organizations that market their programs commercially (including, on occasion, Extension and other university units), and the organizations will often conform their evaluations to meet the required methodological standards.

Evaluator Expertise. Consideration of methodological options may be limited by the expertise, preferences, or proclivities of the individual evaluator leading the project. Evaluators may have strong tendencies toward quantitative or qualitative approaches. They may prefer certain measurement strategies or analytical methods. For example, some Extension evaluators make frequent use of retrospective pretests as an alternative to multiple measurement sessions, while others are skeptical of the strategy. These individual preferences may naturally be reflected in planning decisions about methods.

Organizational Culture. Finally, we turn to the influence of the larger organization. The organization that sponsors a program typically has built up a set of expectations for what evaluations should accomplish or how they should be designed. This could arise from the directives of individual administrators, managers, or evaluation offices (see Chapter Four), or it could develop from structural elements of the organization such as the location of Extension within the academic environment of land-grant universities. The next section examines this topic in greater detail.

Methodological Rigor and the Implementing Organization

The potential variations in standards about rigor and evidence can sometimes be seen as a reflection of organizational culture. Community-based programs are often the product of sponsoring organizations—universities, government agencies, philanthropic foundations, and so forth—that are committed to creating, refining, renewing, and occasionally discarding individual programs, with the overall goal of serving audiences ever more effectively and efficiently. Over a period of years, programs are in a state of constant change, reflecting the advancement of theory and methodology, as well as society's shifting priorities. Indeed, Trochim (2007) has drawn a parallel between the evolution of programs and Darwinian principles of natural selection among organisms and species. An organization's culture can include an expectation of the evidentiary processes that will underlie that evolution, as well as the processes through which specific decisions are reached in individual program evaluations. Organizational expectations can be summarized in several fundamental questions:

- *From where do the standards of rigor derive?* The organizational leadership generally determines the expectations for what the program will accomplish—usually phrased in the language of impact or outcomes—but, the standards for what is acceptable with regard to measurement, design, and other elements are often left to the evaluators to determine. Alternatively, in cases that involve grant funding, the standards for evaluation rigor may be specified directly in the request for applications or the grant award instructions.

- *How are the decisions about evaluation methodology made?* These decisions, illustrated earlier in Table 6.1, may be based on a variety of considerations involving available methods choices, with the goal of meeting the standards in a cost-efficient way. There are numerous advantages to convening an interactive stakeholder process to address these considerations, as Patton (2008) describes. More frequently, however, the program stakeholders may defer to the evaluator's judgments about the sequence of decisions and expect the evaluator to inform them about how the evaluation study will proceed.

- *How, and to what extent, is the quality of a completed evaluation determined?* Once an evaluation has been completed, various stakeholders may find it difficult to ascertain the validity of claims regarding the evaluation's strength of evidence—for example, whether the results do or do not provide evidence of program impact. Those interpretations require technical acumen, as well as time and willingness to delve into the study for a thorough inspection. Administrators may be much more inclined to take evaluators or analysts at their word. However, the most appropriate conclusions may be multidimensional and nuanced. For example, will the achievement of an intermediate outcome that is moderately correlated with the longer-term outcome justify a claim of high impact? Are the characteristics of the evaluation sample in alignment with the extent to which the impact claim is being generalized? Have statistical tests been used appropriately? In some organizations, the expertise needed to answer such questions may reside only in the evaluator who produced the evaluation. In other cases there may be an evaluation or research office that can review the evaluation report and the study's methodology.

Organizations differ with respect to which offices or individuals are given responsibility for addressing these questions and for maintaining the organization's standards of rigor. In many cases—perhaps the great majority—this responsibility falls to the evaluator. Nevertheless the benefits of evaluation and the process of organizational learning are strengthened if these discussions can be extended to a broader group of the organization's administrators and decision makers.

The Evaluator's Role in Ensuring Rigor Within the Organization

The evaluation generally entails resource expenditures and potential program disruptions, but in numerous ways it is expected to produce benefits down the road in terms of the program's increased quality, visibility, and sustainability. The evaluation planning team needs to assess the appropriate balance between acceptable costs and later benefits, and it needs to make decisions accordingly. In light of his or her expertise and experience, the evaluator will typically have the clearest sense of what a successful balance is between methodological requirements and the demands on participants and staff. Ultimately the decisions must rest with the planning team rather than the evaluator alone, but this part of the process requires skillful leadership on the part of the evaluator to maximize the opportunity for the evaluation to be useful or influential.

Evaluators working within organizations also have a significant opportunity to help promote organizational learning with regard to development and implementation of programs. Overall, for the long-term evolution of their organizations, we see evaluators as being able to contribute five distinct functions.

Educating Stakeholders About the Criteria for Evaluation Decisions. This function refers to the need to develop a shared sense among stakeholders about what constitutes acceptable evidence and how that evidence can be used for the ultimate benefit of the program, whether in terms of improved decision making, effective program advocacy, or informal learning and discussion.

Negotiation or Coordination of the Decision-Making Process. Evaluators typically need to lead the process of identifying specific methods-related decisions and the available options for each (as illustrated in Table 6.1), as well as choosing those options that best meet the criteria, given available resources. For example, in planning for a survey of community perceptions the evaluator may stress the need for a formal sampling strategy even though program staff, community partners, or other stakeholders may desire a convenience sample, which they see as simpler, faster, cheaper, and easier to implement.

Interpretation of Findings After Data Collection Has Been Completed. The methodological characteristics of an evaluation allow certain kinds of conclusions to be drawn from the data and largely determine the confidence levels that can be ascribed to the findings. They also constrain how broadly the study's conclusions can be generalized to other settings and populations. Discussion about what recommendations may be justified by the results, especially if stakeholders are partisan to the program, may lose sight of the strength of the evidence. The evaluator can facilitate this interpretation process and try to make sure that findings are not over- or under-interpreted.

Defense of the Evaluation Methodology. Evaluations might also be criticized, sometimes forcefully. Countering this criticism may be particularly important in cases where controversy exists about either the program or the problem it is intended to address. For example, individuals who are opposed to a program on ideological grounds may seek to disparage the adequacy of the evaluation, and the effectiveness of the program, as the most politically expedient approach for arguing against continuation. In such cases the evaluator is in the best position to promote an objective assessment of the evaluation's strengths and weaknesses, and to delineate why the methodological choices made were the best available. As Chelimsky (2007) describes, sometimes evaluators must also take the lead in countering inflexible institutional biases toward specific methodologies such as experimental designs.

Long-Term Education of the Organization. Over time, the sponsoring organization can be guided to develop a thoughtful and consistent approach to the evaluation process, in terms of relevant expectations, value systems, resource expenditures, and contributions to decision making. As discussed earlier, evaluation criteria differ across specific programs, but these individual cases may share commonalities reflecting the philosophy and culture of the larger organization. In addition, a basic literacy about the evaluation process can be built among the organization's administrators and staff. The evaluator can play a central role in promoting this process of organizational learning (Preskill & Torres, 1999; Russ-Eft & Preskill, 2001).

Examples From the Cooperative Extension System

Cooperative Extension programs present an ideal context in which to examine and illustrate these processes, because of Extension's organizational complexity, diverse local programming, and disparate stakeholders. Extension programs are delivered in an environment marked by high public visibility, ongoing funding concerns, and several levels of government. For a given Extension program, the relevant stakeholders may include program funders, program participants, state agencies, community-based organizations, state legislators, federal Extension partners, county Extension staff, campus administrators, and campus departments. Frequently, the challenges are compounded because programs are delivered at multiple sites, in different regions of a state. In these cases, a consistency in methodology across sites (or alternatively, a planned series of variations) is not easy to achieve.

We present two examples from Extension practice that illustrate the role of methodological rigor in evaluation planning and utilization. The first reflects a high level of rigor; the second reflects a more moderate level that is still consistent with the purposes of the evaluation and available resources. In both cases, the planning process produced evaluations of high visibility and usefulness that were responsive to primary stakeholder concerns.

The California EFNEP Evaluation. The Expanded Food and Nutrition Education Program (EFNEP) was launched in 1968 by the USDA to help low-income families maintain a nutritious diet within a limited household budget. In 1979, there was little previous impact evaluation of EFNEP, and University of California Cooperative Extension undertook a major evaluation of its statewide EFNEP program with the intent of determining whether, and how, the program was achieving its intended effects. With funding from a USDA grant, the California team proceeded to conduct the study with a high level of rigor, to allow conclusions to be drawn with strong confidence.

The evaluation used a waitlist control group design in which participants in 15 California counties were recruited to the program and randomly assigned to either the treatment or control condition. The measures included questionnaires that addressed 24-hour food recall as well as food-related behaviors, attitudes, and knowledge. Data were collected through personal interviews conducted by trained program assistants who were also teachers in the program.

Complete pretest-posttest data were obtained for 683 participants. The evaluation concluded that the program produced improvements in a large number of indicators, including planning and shopping for meals, cooking skills, food safety, consumption of fruits and vegetables, and nutrition knowledge, among others. Program effectiveness was tied to the number of home visits, the length of the visits, and the instruction topics. (See Block, Laughlin, Del Tredici, & Omelich, 1985, for further details.)

High standards for methodological rigor were evident in all phases of the study. For example, the instruments were developed through a thorough process of pilot testing and reliability assessment. The nutrition aides serving as interviewers did not collect data from any of the participants whom they taught in the program, in order to control potential interviewer-related bias. Participant attrition from the study (about 38% overall) was analyzed to assess whether it may have occurred differentially across conditions; it was determined that attrition was fairly evenly distributed and did not appear to be a source of bias.

This carefully conducted evaluation study made an important contribution to the evolving perception—at both the state and national levels—that EFNEP is an effective and valuable program for serving the nutrition-related needs of disadvantaged families. The study was published in a leading journal (Del Tredici, Joy, Omelich, & Laughlin, 1988), which served to enhance its visibility and credibility with audiences from academic, administrative, and policy backgrounds. In addition, the study's insights about learning processes led to structural changes in the educational program, with regard to standardizing the number and duration of lessons.

In large part because of numerous rigorous evaluations conducted over the years at the national and state levels (CSREES, 2007), EFNEP has come to be recognized as an important federal investment (see, for example, Randall, Brink, & Joy, 1989). In sum, the California evaluation was successful in advancing both the EFNEP program and the field of nutrition education, and the highly rigorous approach to design, implementation, and analysis was an essential component of its success.

The Minnesota 4-H Youth Survey. The Minnesota 4-H Youth Development Program conducted a survey of 4-H members in winter 2002, as part of a larger evaluation on the program's impact on youths in the state (Minnesota 4-H Program, 2005). The primary goal of the evaluation was to examine alignment of the program with its underlying program theory model, which identifies eight program components and six developmental outcomes as critical to the 4-H program's success. The survey was also conducted to produce a base of evidence for the value of the 4-H program in Minnesota, with relevant audiences including legislators, state and local agencies, and Extension administrators. To help focus the study and decide on its design elements, the evaluators convened an advisory committee that included university researchers, youth, and program volunteers.

The questionnaire items assessed members' 4-H involvement, school-related experiences, time use outside of school, social support, use of technology, and involvement in risk behaviors. The evaluation team did not consider it feasible to establish a comparison group, so the design called for participants' responses to be compared to responses from a 2001 statewide general population student survey conducted by the Minnesota Department of Education (2007). Questionnaires were sent out to a randomly selected sample of 575 Minnesota 4-H members in grades 7 through 12, and 257 questionnaires were returned.

The survey results produced an impressive profile of 4-H youths compared to the general population in the state. 4-H members reported significantly higher levels of prosocial behaviors and significantly lower involvement in risk behaviors compared to the statewide figures. However, in light of the limited comparability between the 4-H survey and the statewide survey, no claims were made that the 4-H program was responsible for these differences.

The results were posted online (Minnesota 4-H Program, 2005) and disseminated to stakeholder audiences in Minnesota. In their communications, the evaluators paid careful attention to the methodological limitations of their data. For example, the demographic characteristics of respondents and nonrespondents were compared, which was particularly important in light of the response rate of 44.7%. Those analyses revealed that longtime 4-H members responded at a higher rate than newer members did, potentially limiting the representativeness of the responding sample. These concerns are discussed on the 4-H Program's Web site, along with the implications for data interpretation. The discussion of methodology and rigor is presented in terms appropriate for a nontechnical audience.

From the perspective of our preceding discussion, we would assess the Minnesota study's level of rigor as fully appropriate for its evaluation purposes. The results showed an intriguing profile of 4-H youth, although the evaluation design was not equipped to address questions about program causality or change over time in targeted characteristics of the adolescents. The evaluators did not overinterpret their data, and they used the evaluation as only one of several forms of information from which to consider the value of the 4-H program. The commitment to working through the initial evaluation plan with an advisory committee promoted acceptance of the methodological decisions and their limitations. With respect to utilization, the evaluation was well-received within the state and contributed to discussions with legislators and other audiences. Those discussions contributed to the 4-H youth development program's success in obtaining local funding for critical program coordinator positions in several Minnesota counties (M. Marczak, personal communication, April 2008).

Conclusions

We have presented a case for considering methodological rigor as the product of numerous evaluation planning decisions that are tied to the desired strength of confidence in the evaluation's conclusions, while also taking into account costs and other factors. These decisions should be arrived at through reflection and consultation, with attention to the intended purposes of the evaluation, stakeholders' information needs, various categories of cost, and the available resources. Within complex organizational settings such as the Extension system, evaluators have several essential leadership tasks: they can lead the planning process for determining a study's design and methodology, they can represent and defend those decisions in the programmatic and administrative arenas as the evaluation is interpreted and used, and over the long run they can educate their organization about the specific benefits and the realistic costs of conducting rigorous evaluations. Evaluations do not need to conform to perceived standards of methodology that may be unrelated to the requirements of the specific program setting. However, good evaluations do need to stand up to careful examination about what we have learned and how we have learned it. Methodological rigor is at the center of such discussion, and careful examination needs to be promoted and encouraged in the process of building learning organizations.

References

Bennett, C. F., & Rockwell, K. (1996). *Targeting Outcomes of Programs (TOP): An integrated approach to planning and evaluation.* Washington, DC: CSREES, USDA.

Block, A., Laughlin, S., Del Tredici, A., & Omelich, C. (1985). *California EFNEP Evaluation Study.* Berkeley: Cooperative Extension, University of California Division of Agriculture and Natural Resources.

Braverman, M. T. (1996). Sources of survey error: Implications for evaluation studies. In M. T. Braverman & J. K. Slater (Eds.), *Advances in survey research. New Directions for Evaluation, 70,* 17–28.

Chatterji, M. (2007). Grades of evidence: Variability in quality of findings in effectiveness studies of complex field interventions. *American Journal of Evaluation, 28*(3), 239–255.

Chelimsky, E. (2007). Factors influencing the choice of methods in federal evaluation practice. In G. Julnes & D. J. Rog (Eds.), *Informing federal policies on evaluation methodology. New Directions for Evaluation, 113*, 13–33.

Cooperative State Research, Education, and Extension Service. (2007). *Research studies of the Expanded Food and Nutrition Education Program: 1989–2006.* U.S. Department of Agriculture. Retrieved April 11, 2008, from http://www.csrees.usda.gov/nea/food/efnep/pdf/research_studies.pdf

Del Tredici, A. M., Joy, A. B., Omelich, C. L., & Laughlin, S. G. (1988). Evaluation study of the California Expanded Food and Nutrition Education Program: 24-hour food recall data. *Journal of the American Dietetic Association, 88*(2), 185–190.

Dennis, M. L. (1994). Ethical and practical randomized field experiments. In J. S. Wholey, H. P. Hatry, & K. E. Newcomer (Eds.), *Handbook of practical program evaluation* (pp. 155–197). San Francisco: Jossey-Bass.

Institute of Education Sciences. (2008). *What Works Clearinghouse.* Retrieved April 12, 2008, from http://ies.ed.gov/ncee/wwc/

Lipsey, M. W. (1993). Theory as method: Small theories of treatments. In L. B. Sechrest & A.G. Scott (Eds.), *Understanding causes and generalizing about them. New Directions for Program Evaluation, 57*, 5–38.

Lipsey, M. W. (1998). Design sensitivity: Statistical power for applied experimental research. In L. Bickman & D. J. Rog (Eds.), *Handbook of applied social research methods* (pp. 39–68). Thousand Oaks, CA: Sage.

Minnesota Department of Education. (2007). *Minnesota Student Survey.* Retrieved April 11, 2008, from http://education.state.mn.us/MDE/Learning_Support/Safe_and_Healthy_Learners/Minnesota_Student_Survey

Minnesota 4-H Program. (2005). *Minnesota 4-H Youth Survey.* Retrieved April 11, 2008, from http://www.fourh.umn.edu/evaluation/evaluating/youthsurvey.html

Patton, M. Q. (2008). *Utilization-focused evaluation* (4th ed.). Thousand Oaks, CA: Sage.

Preskill, H., & Torres, R. T. (1999). *Evaluative inquiry for learning in organizations.* Thousand Oaks, CA: Sage.

Randall, M. J., Brink, M. S., & Joy, A. B. (1989). EFNEP: An investment in America's future. *Journal of Nutrition Education, 21*(6), 276–279.

Rogers, P. J., Hacsi, T. A., Petrosino, A., & Huebner, T. A. (Eds.). (2000). *Program theory in evaluation: Challenges and opportunities. New Directions for Evaluation, 87.*

Russ-Eft, D., & Preskill, H. (2001). *Evaluation in organizations: A systematic approach to enhancing learning, performance, and change.* Cambridge, MA: Perseus.

Schweigert, F. J. (2006). The meaning of effectiveness in assessing community initiatives. *American Journal of Evaluation, 27*(4), 416–436.

Shadish, W. R., Cook, T. D., & Campbell D. T. (2002). *Experimental and quasi-experimental designs for generalized causal inference.* Boston: Houghton-Mifflin.

Society for Prevention Research. (2004). *Standards of evidence: Criteria for efficacy, effectiveness and dissemination.* Retrieved February 9, 2008, from http://www.preventionresearch.org/StandardsofEvidencebook.pdf

St. Pierre, R. G. (2004). Using randomized experiments. In J. S. Wholey, H. P. Hatry, & K. E. Newcomer (Eds.), *Handbook of practical program evaluation* (2nd ed., pp. 150–175). San Francisco: Jossey-Bass.

Substance Abuse and Mental Health Services Administration. (2008). *National Registry of Evidence-based Programs and Practices.* Retrieved April 12, 2008, from http://nrepp.samhsa.gov/

Trochim, W. (2007). *Evolutionary perspectives in evaluation: Theoretical and practical implications.* Retrieved February 9, 2008, from http://www.socialresearchmethods.net/

research/EERS2007/Evolutionary%20Perspectives%20in%20Evaluation%20Theoretical%
20and%20Practical%20Implications.pdf
Weiss, C. H., Murphy-Graham, E., Petrosino, A., & Gandhi, A. G. (2008). The Fairy
Godmother—and her warts: Making the dream of evidence-based policy come true.
American Journal of Evaluation, 29(1), 29–47.

MARC T. BRAVERMAN *is the associate dean for extension and outreach in the
College of Health and Human Sciences, program leader of the Extension
Family and Community Development Program, and a professor of human devel-
opment and family sciences at Oregon State University.*

MARY E. ARNOLD *is an associate professor and 4-H youth development specialist
with the Oregon State University Extension Service, whose work involves teaching and conducting evaluations with the Oregon 4-H program.*

NEW DIRECTIONS FOR EVALUATION • DOI: 10.1002/ev

Duttweiler, M. W. (2008). The value of evaluation in Cooperative Extension. In M. T.
Braverman, M. Engle, M. E. Arnold, & R. A. Rennekamp (Eds.), *Program evaluation in a
complex organizational system: Lessons from Cooperative Extension. New Directions for Evaluation, 120*, 87–100.

The Value of Evaluation
in Cooperative Extension

Michael W. Duttweiler

Abstract

*The author considers whether current evaluation practice is of value to the
Cooperative Extension System. Evaluation use and influence in Extension are
characterized through literature review and examination of case examples
informed by correspondence with study authors. The more than 675 evaluations examined consistently yielded specific and valuable program counsel
applicable to Extension education practice. Nearly seven in ten studies
addressed at least one aspect of program improvement. Beyond simply
generating a supply of potentially useful findings, there was clear evidence of
substantive program modification in response to program evaluation. Case
examples indicated that evaluation studies have influenced Extension practice
by helping to establish program direction, improving existing educational practice, informing public policy, establishing or sustaining program support, establishing a basis for resource allocation decisions, influencing relationships with
stakeholders, and strengthening evaluation practice itself. The author concludes
that evaluation practice is both dynamic and influential within the Cooperative Extension System. © Wiley Periodicals, Inc.*

The core question addressed in this chapter is whether current evaluation practice is of value to the Cooperative Extension System. The task of characterizing evaluation use across a system of more than 100 academic institutions engaged in content areas ranging from financial literacy for limited resource families to genomics-based technology transfer is a formidable challenge. For the purposes of this chapter, two data sources regarding evaluation activity are employed: review of published program evaluation studies and peer nomination of highly influential evaluation studies. This exploration focuses on the views about evaluation practice of Extension educators rather than of those formally charged with leadership for program evaluation. In other words, how do educators directly involved in developing and implementing Extension educational programs employ evaluation, and to what ends? Standard accountability reporting, although obviously essential for organizational survival, is not a primary focus.

Evaluation Practice as Reflected Through Published Evaluation Studies

Review of published evaluation studies was the first source considered for characterizing evaluation use. The task is more complicated than it might seem because there are many venues for publishing the results of these studies. For example, an educator working in parent education might publish a program evaluation report in the journal *Family Relations* or the *Journal of Marriage and Family,* while an agricultural economics educator might publish in *Agricultural Economics* or the *Journal of Rural Studies.* Dozens of formal publishing outlets come into play, to say nothing of in-house publications. Fortunately, there is one publishing venue employed by a range of Extension education professionals, the *Journal of Extension.* As indicated on the *Journal's* Web site (Journal of Extension, 2007), *JOE* is the official refereed journal of the Cooperative Extension System. It seeks to "expand and update the research and knowledge base for Extension professionals and other adult educators to improve their effectiveness." Review of published evaluation studies in *JOE* was the first means to examine Cooperative Extension System evaluation practice.

This examination involved a review of articles published in the journal over the past 10 years (1998–2007). The process was intentional if not precise. Roughly 2,000 articles appeared in the 60 issues published over that time period. Obviously not all described the results of evaluation studies. To select articles for review, the definition used for *program evaluation study* was any work that involved "the systematic acquisition and assessment of information to provide useful feedback about some object" (Trochim, 1999). To be included in this review, articles had to expressly reference acquisition and use of programmatic information. Consequently, items not considered included commentaries on evaluation needs or methods without reference to supporting evaluation data, applied research reports in content areas that

NEW DIRECTIONS FOR EVALUATION • DOI: 10.1002/ev

might inform extension curricula but that did not specifically address educational processes, and descriptions of evaluation resources or methods without reference to application data.

Each *JOE* issue presents brief abstracts with links to the full text. The abstracts were used for initial screening. Although the criterion "information acquisition and assessment" was applied broadly, some additional "evaluation studies" likely were missed by using the abstracts as a screening mechanism. Even so, 669 articles published in the 10-year period met the definition used. Once selected, articles were reviewed in detail and characterized by program content area, identified purposes, geographic scope, form(s) of evaluation employed, and state of origin of the lead author. The latter was used as a coarse indicator of how representative the articles were of the nationwide Extension system. In addition, each study was assigned a "level of evaluation" adapted from Jacobs (1988): (1) needs assessment, (2) program documentation, (3) program fidelity (comparisons of program intent to actuality), (4) program improvement, and (5) evidence of effectiveness. In the case of studies with blended levels of evaluation, the level assigned was the one judged to be dominant, on the basis of the full article text.

A basic question is whether articles published in *JOE* are representative of the entire Extension system. Over the course of the 10-year period, 48 states were represented, although four had only one or two articles each and two institutions accounted for 20% of all articles selected. Both of the latter institutions have strong support for evaluation practice, as well as promotion and tenure systems in place for field-based faculty that include explicit expectations for publishing. The top 10 institutions in terms of frequency of submission accounted for nearly 50% of all articles selected. Clearly, it is not appropriate to expect observations based on *JOE* article review to predict practice at a given institution, but a broad range of organizational contexts is represented.

A typical evaluation study from the *JOE* collection was situated in either the youth development or agriculture and food systems program areas, had the dual purpose of outcome documentation and educational process improvement, was statewide in scope, and employed simple survey methodology. Although studies focused on youth development or agriculture and food systems accounted for nearly half of all those reported, there were also numerous examples from rural economic development, nutrition and health, family and consumer sciences, and natural resources and environment. About one in eight studies applied across content areas, focusing on topics such as organizational marketing, adoption of electronic technology by educators, and professional development needs of educators. Organization administrators and educators in all content areas clearly employ program evaluation for multiple purposes.

There was significant variation in both evaluation level and stated purpose of evaluation. Referring to the level of evaluation, program improvement at 40% and evidence of effectiveness at 35% dominated. Needs assessment accounted for nearly all of the remaining 25%. Program improvement and needs assessment likely are promoted by the self-interest of practitioners and the organization, while external accountability demands often drive effectiveness evaluation. It is interesting that only a handful of studies focused on program documentation or program fidelity. Perhaps both are addressed through less formal methods, but this could also indicate a meaningful gap in evaluation practice.

Evaluation purposes articulated by study authors were also noted. They were found to closely follow the assigned level of evaluation but were somewhat more specific. Categories used to classify evaluation purposes emerged from review of the cases. The categories populated by at least 10 studies are identified in Table 7.1.

Tallying the purposes assigned to level 4 (program improvement) indicates that nearly seven in ten studies involved at least some element of program improvement. Program management and improvement by practitioners appear to be very strong motivators indeed for evaluation studies within Extension.

In terms of geographic scope, the studies were dominated by statewide surveys, which constituted 52% of the total, while about 32% were restricted to specific venues in which the program was delivered (one or more local sites). Of the balance, about 10% covered multicounty or in-state regions, and 6% covered multistate regions. Multistate evaluation reports increased in recent years, perhaps signaling growing collaboration to address evaluation needs or response to pressure from federal funders to increase multistate approaches.

Table 7.1. Distribution of *Journal of Extension* **Studies by Specific Evaluation Purpose and by Jacobs's Levels of Evaluation**

Evaluation Purpose	Percentage Citing Purpose[a]	Level of Evaluation[b]
Educational methods improvement	48	4
Accountability studies (including outcome and impact studies)	41	5
Needs assessment	32	1
Professional development or staffing needs	11	4
Audience analysis	6	1
Improvement of internal operations	6	4
Curriculum design	4	4
Customer satisfaction assessment	2	5
Marketing studies	2	1

[a]Total N (JOE studies from 1998–2007 meeting selection criteria): 669.

[b]Code (from Jacobs, 1988): 1 = Needs assessment; 2 = Program documentation; 3 = Program fidelity; 4 = Program improvement; 5 = Evidence of effectiveness.

New Directions for Evaluation • DOI: 10.1002/ev

The last characterization of the published studies was by evaluation methods employed. Taken as a whole, the methods mix can be seen as not very rich. Single-point-in-time standard survey methodology strongly dominated, at 66% of the reported studies. However, about one in four of the studies employing standard surveys also incorporated at least one other method. The next most common forms of data gathering were pre- and posttesting (10%), focus groups (9%), and various forms of qualitative interviews (8%). Use of qualitative methods increased modestly across the sampling period and represented about 25% of the studies in total. In terms of evaluation design, only 4% included formally identified comparison or control groups, and a similar proportion described some form of longitudinal assessment.

Review of published studies thus reveals the dominance of practical and modest evaluation efforts addressing specific organizational needs, for the purpose of enhancing programs and organizational structures and processes within which the programs reside. With this characterization in hand, we move next to exploring the specific influences and benefits of evaluation studies to the Cooperative Extension System.

Utilization and Influence of Evaluation Studies

Does evaluation in fact have a strong influence on Extension education practice in the Cooperative Extension System? Each published study has a story to tell regarding use and utility of evaluation findings, likely representing the full spectrum from highly valued to quickly forgotten. Utility of any particular study might be evidenced in a number of ways, such as influence on program direction, improvement of existing educational practices, informed public policy, established or sustained program support, elimination of ineffective programs, strengthened relationships with stakeholders, or enhanced evaluation practice itself.

Specific influences of evaluation studies within the Cooperative Extension System were explored by considering a small collection of evaluation studies in more detail. The studies were selected in two ways: purposeful selection during review of *Journal of Extension* articles and requests to Extension evaluator colleagues across the system to identify specific evaluations that in their view were highly valued and influential.

Nine evaluation studies are described here to illustrate a range of evaluation influences and contexts. Primary selection criteria were the degree to which specific implications of the study were articulated and whether follow-up application was described. Beyond that, the cases were chosen to address a range of evaluation uses, with emphasis on instrumental use to improve program structure and function and conceptual use to educate decision makers (Clavijo, Fleming, Hoermann, Toal, & Johnson, 2005). Lead authors of the studies were contacted to ascertain whether the evaluations had generated specific changes in Extension practice.

Organizational structure can determine whether a programmatic relationship with communities even gets off the ground. In our first example, Weerts (2005) explored university-community collaborations to determine the critical factors in establishing and sustaining effective partnerships. The programs involved were sustained partnerships between universities and communities in three states. Common factors that emerged as influential in demonstrating institutional commitment to the community were language and symbolic actions of campus leadership, personal experiences with faculty and staff, and success in navigating the complex structures of the university. All three factors relate to structure and implementation of effective partnerships and have practical implications for program development. Although the analytical framework of the study and initial findings focused on specific actions to initiate and sustain campus-community partnerships, findings as a whole demonstrated clear need for an organizational culture in support of outreach and engagement.

In follow-up correspondence, Weerts noted that as a faculty member not directly involved in a formal outreach system connected to other institutions, it is somewhat challenging to know what influence the study has had (D. J. Weerts, personal communication, April 1, 2008). For the cases in his study, feedback was given directly to the program partners for their consideration and use. In addition, results were shared widely at outreach scholarship conferences. In the case of his home institution, the findings informed a university strategic planning process. Specifically, a strategic goal related to community responsiveness and relationships was expanded beyond technology or information transfer to consideration of reciprocal partnerships. Thus the study illustrated both instrumental and conceptual application of evaluation findings as defined by Clavijo et al. (2005).

Assessing the effectiveness of collaborative efforts is particularly challenging. Aguilar and Thornsbury (2005) explored the role of Extension in delivering appropriate and reliable information as input to the decision-making process of clientele groups via a case study of work with the Michigan Apple Committee. A key dimension of the study context was that program recipients were also the direct sponsors of the program. The evaluation presented information useful to the committee in assessing its own effectiveness, as perceived by its members, and also informed Extension program staff about their effectiveness in supporting the group. Thus the intent was to strengthen the evaluation capacity of both the collaborating group and Extension itself. Key elements of the approach included explaining the advantages and disadvantages of chosen evaluation methods, establishing realistic expectations for the evaluation process, and articulating the intended use of the findings to inform future decisions. The importance of mutually agreed evaluation purposes, careful exploration of issues identified, and specific interpretation of findings was reinforced. Aguilar and Thornsbury noted, "The proactive participation and empowerment of group leaders are required to guarantee that research tools used will gather information that is needed to make decisions" (paragraph 6). It was clear that evaluation capacity building had to extend beyond the organization's leadership team to include organization members, to ensure appropriate use of findings and sustain future evaluation practice.

Study author Thornsbury (S. D. Thornsbury, personal communication, March 13, 2008) indicates that the educators involved "have definitely changed how we do our work and how we approach problems." Thornsbury goes on, though, to articulate the challenge of separating the effect of a given evaluation study from other influences. "What is the influence of one study and how do you separate that from other studies, or even just from the reflection of an educator who realizes that different outcomes are needed perhaps and maybe even ideally before users are even able to articulate those outcomes?" In subsequent correspondence, Thornsbury (personal communication, March 24, 2008) notes that the study itself indicated a change in how Extension professionals do their work, reflecting the need to more carefully plan and document programs and their impacts, and comments, "This is driven in large part by resource constraints, both on the Cooperative Extension System itself and on clientele groups we serve." Relative to changes the study prompted in the clientele group, the published summary reports some shift toward acceptance of a broader range of supported research projects. Thornsbury notes, "It has not been a rapid or radical change by any means, but does continue to grow year-by-year."

As an organization with a public mission that receives public support, it is essential that Extension programs effectively target diverse audiences. More than a dozen studies appearing in *JOE* in the past five years explored how program methods and content are accepted across audiences and audience segments. Gregory et al. (2006) examined volunteerism within programming for Latino communities in five diverse California settings. The impetus for the study was typical among many studies reviewed: there was a performance gap in current efforts. Specifically, established approaches for recruiting volunteers to support youth programming were not working satisfactorily in Latino communities. The study was facilitated greatly by identifying credible community liaisons to supply context and recruit participants, establishing a credible relationship between the researchers and the community. Recommended strategies for organizations that seek to deliver programs to youths and families were explored through interviews of Latino adults identified as either participants or nonparticipants in specific program activities.

Results indicated that traditional approaches for recruiting adult volunteers should be reframed significantly to emphasize "helping" the community, and that there was need for multiple, flexible opportunities for involvement. Practical strategies were identified for strengthening volunteer recruitment and support. Lead author Gregory (P. Gregory, personal communication, March 12, 2008) reports that one result of this project was production of a guide for partnering with Latino communities, which has been widely distributed to Extension offices in California for staff use and as a training tool for other agencies.

Many Extension programs aim to strengthen community resources available to address the needs of specific audiences. Suarez-Balcazar, Martinez, Cox, and Jayraj (2006) explored the role of farmers' markets in addressing nutritional needs of African Americans not met by local food stores. In addition to collecting direct feedback from market participants, comparative need and opportunity were assessed by considering fresh produce availability in a comparison community with similar demographics. Although significant satisfaction existed among those using the farmers' markets, many opportunities to strengthen local markets were identified. The study examined features of markets in low-income communities compared to other communities and identified important differences in operations and product availability. Potential roles for Extension in establishing and sustaining farmers' markets were outlined. Of note was the fact that identified roles extended well beyond consumers to the farming community and the supports that need to be in place to sustain a viable farmers' market. Once again, an evaluation focused on a specific educational program strategy surfaced implications far beyond, including policy and infrastructure concerns.

In terms of direct effect on the target community, author Suarez-Balcazar reports little change in availability of farmers' markets to African American communities (Y. Suarez-Balcazar, personal communication, March 12, 2008). However, this study was part of a larger set of studies looking at food security, school luncheon programs, and food access (Suarez-Balcazar et al., 2006) which have made "important contributions to the understanding of the problem of access to healthy foods" (p. 112) in working-class African American communities, contributing important strategies for dealing with food insecurity.

The focus of the next study (Perkins & Mincemoyer, 2007) was to determine if youths who participate in the 4-H Youth Development Program show an increase in life skill development over time. Acquisition of valuable life skills is a primary rationale for the sustained relationship with youths that 4-H can provide. Nearly 1,200 young people in Pennsylvania State University 4-H programs were tracked over a four-year period. Each completed a "Skills for Everyday Living" assessment before and after involvement. This assessment is a good example of how evaluation practice is strengthened by collaboration across the Cooperative Extension System. This validated assessment approach was developed as part of a national initiative to measure the impact of youth development programs (Mincemoyer & Perkins, 2005). Authors of the Pennsylvania study concluded that "youth's ability in the five life skills measured—decision making, critical thinking, communication, goal setting, and problem solving—was significantly greater after their participation in the 4-H program than before they started the program."

NEW DIRECTIONS FOR EVALUATION • DOI: 10.1002/ev

   Author Perkins (D. F. Perkins, personal communication, March 17, 2008) indicates that the initial study led to establishment of an online system for data collection, the products of which are being used for accountability and marketing, program management, performance management, professional development, and curriculum development. Data collected annually are aggregated into a one-page statewide impact sheet used with state-level legislators to make the case for 4-H Youth Development programming. A significant number of 4-H educators are using the system because the value to them is clear. Individual educators are given data indicating trends in performance across the life skill areas as a basis for active program management. Educators can also generate short impact statements for local accountability and marketing. Some educators are including results summaries as part of their promotion dossiers. Hands-on training in use of the data collection system is incorporated in annual training, and educators using the pre- and posttest capabilities are beginning to make curricular adjustments based on results. Perkins reports that even early naysayers have expressed that they "really need and use the data."
   The next example, while also focusing on 4-H youth development, differs from the Perkins and Mincemoyer (2007) case by exploring one statewide program in depth. Taylor-Powell and Calvert (2006) describe assessment of the longstanding arts program of the University of Wisconsin Extension 4-H Youth Development program, which reaches about 19,000 youths annually via more than 80 activities in the visual, performing, and communication arts across the state. The study was conducted by a team of state specialists, county educators, and youths. The team identified twelve relevant youth development outcomes that became the framework for a statewide survey of program participants. These quantitative data were supplemented by focus groups and qualitative interviewing. Results indicated that the visual and communication arts program generated strong positive results, particularly in the developmental areas of mastery and independence. Program characteristics critical to sustained program success were identified. Characteristics that distinguished the program from other arts and communication offerings were also documented, notably the mix of participants, freedom of choice within the program, and the positive and supportive learning environment generated by the program.
   When author Taylor-Powell (E. Taylor-Powell, personal communication, December 1, 2007) was asked what the specific values or benefits of the study were, she identified improved impact reporting, active program improvement, and sustained support. Specifically, the statewide program leader had available clear quantitative and qualitative data to use in briefings with key stakeholders and in impact reporting. The state coordinator of the arts and communication program found similar information valuable but also gained greater understanding of program effects and areas for improvement. County-based staff benefited from impact data, increased understanding of program strengths and needs for improvement, including

ways to target the program more effectively. Resulting sustained financing for arts and communication programs and program improvements has directly benefited participating youths. Lastly, those involved with the study process felt validated and rewarded, and new partners were identified. When asked what specific aspects or attributes of the evaluation led to its utility, Taylor-Powell identified use of an existing research base, engagement of educators and administration in design and implementation of the study, effort spent in identifying useful indicators, ongoing communications with educators and those involved in the evaluation, the collaborative nature of the evaluation process, and efforts to "package" and use the results in reports, briefings, presentations, and Web documents.

The studies described here typically focus on documentation of impact and identification of opportunities for program improvement. It seems naïve to assume that program evaluation studies by themselves are likely to lead to substantive programmatic change. As noted by Sandison (2006), "The utilisation of evaluation, and any other learning tool, is essentially a study of the nature of change. This is not under the control of any one person or process. The more complex the use, the more that this is so. Arguably, the evaluation is but a catalyst." However, the next example illustrates the powerful role evaluation can play as a catalyst for change well beyond the initial study focus.

The Expanded Food and Nutrition Education Program (EFNEP) is a nationwide nutrition education program directed to needs of limited-resource audiences with the aim of improving nutritional well-being. In the 1970s and 1980s, efforts were undertaken to identify delivery methods that might be more efficient than the traditional one-to-one instructional approach used from the start of the program. Pilot studies in the early 1980s identified no significant differences in learning and behavior outcomes between individual and small-group methods, and a nationwide move toward group instruction ensued (Dollahite & Scott-Pierce, 2003). Noting that the proportion of participants reached via group delivery across New York State had increased steadily from 50% in 1998 to 70% in 2001, Dollahite and Scott-Pierce asked whether that change was consistent with maintaining quality programming and achieving expected outcomes. On examining the original 1981 pilot studies, they discovered that in contrast to current practice, wherein participants were recruited directly to groups, during the pilot tests group instruction was preceded by one-on-one interaction. That prompted a formal look at outcome data for individual and group instruction using standard outcome indicators from the federal reporting system. Dollahite and Scott-Pierce's analysis revealed a significantly lower level of documented outcomes for group-delivered instruction than for one-on-one instruction, contradicting the earlier pilot studies.

According to the lead author (J. Dollahite, personal communication, February 13, 2008), realistic assessment of resources and access to audiences clearly indicated that a return to primarily one-on-one instruction simply was not feasible. This left strengthening group instruction as the primary opportunity for enhancement. Review of instructional approaches and materials in use identified strong nutritional content but limited emphasis on effective group teaching approaches. Consequently, a consultant was hired to help program managers improve their teaching skills. But, it soon became clear that a more fundamental change was needed. Over a five-year period and through a participatory design process, the entire training curriculum for nutrition teaching assistants was shifted from content-driven instructional approaches to those based in learner-focused dialogue. Initially, there was resistance among practitioners and administrators to the new approach, the former due to required changes in practice, the latter due to the expense of retraining an entire workforce. However, the efficacy of the new approach soon became apparent in enhanced results obtained through group instruction. One nutrition teaching assistant observed, "I went kicking and screaming, but it's the best thing I have done since joining [Extension]." Analysis of program effectiveness across methods continues today with evidence of intended outcomes essentially equivalent between individual and group methods. Methods assessment is currently being extended to include cost effectiveness analysis. Thus a modest initial inquiry triggered a series of assessments and program improvements that have substantively strengthened the EFNEP program in New York.

We turn next to a number of recently published studies that focus on strengthening evaluation practice itself. As a local, state, and national organization, the complexities of multilevel evaluation and accountability needs within Extension are daunting (see Chapter Three). Betz and Hill (2006) explored whether standardized evaluation protocols could meet the needs of campus researchers, educators, and community partners. The focal program was the Strengthening Families Program for Parents and Youth in Washington State Extension. The authors noted the particular challenge of addressing differing goal sets of campus researchers and educational practitioners as follows: "The goals of the human science researcher are linked to discovery, confirmation, replication, and dissemination. The youth and family Extension professionals want programs and practices that can be of maximum benefit to the participants, are effective, and can be implemented by a range of staff" (paragraph 4).

Among the questions explored was the value of traditional pretest-posttest and retrospective pretest approaches, as perceived by the various program partners. The importance of ensuring that practitioners and community partners receive and have the opportunity to interact with study findings was noted. Betz and Hill (2006) concluded that evaluation goals of the campus-based researchers and educators could indeed be balanced, that either form of assessment could have value depending on evaluation purposes, and that the key to successful evaluation collaboration was effective engagement of all partners in the overall evaluation process, an approach that has been incorporated in ongoing efforts.

Kelsey, Schnelle, and Bolin (2005) explored evaluation capacity building. They described a multimethod approach for evaluating workshops, a very common instructional mode for Extension, with emphasis on demonstrating values of the evaluation process to Extension professionals, which is fundamental to establishing a culture supportive of program evaluation. The focal program was integrated pest management education. One key to their approach was offering a combination of methods that would inform all phases of the program development process, from needs assessment to instructional design through delivery. Educators were involved in all phases of the evaluation process and could act on results while the program was unfolding. An evaluation consultant was available to assist educators, and a combination of qualitative and quantitative measures was employed. Program participants had multiple opportunities to contribute evaluative feedback. Through their direct involvement, and encouraged by the demonstrated utility of findings, educators invested in developing their own evaluation skills and valued the findings that were generated. The participatory approach, a focus on organizational learning, clear application for program improvement, and long-term benefit to constituents were identified as keys to success.

Lead author Kelsey (K. D. Kelsey, personal communication, March 12, 2008) indicates that a variety of program improvements were made each year based on evaluation results, and that the educators involved came to value evaluation for improving program performance and documenting accountability for annual review and promotion. Kelsey reports that evaluation activity also raised the status of the project among peers by showing that the program was worth the effort and attention of evaluation. Educator and coauthor Schnelle (M. Schnelle, personal communication, March 12, 2008) reports improvements in teaching methods resulting from evaluation, including increasing depth and scope of topics covered and incorporation of take-home materials to supplement face-to-face instruction.

Observations Across Examples

Each of the brief examples given here clearly has value in the context of the decisions at hand—some narrowly confined to a specific program context, some at the level of organizational strategy or even public policy. Several commonalities can be seen across the examples:

- Focus on potential program improvements from the start
- Flexible use of evaluation methods
- Use of participatory methods as appropriate
- Concern about evaluator credibility with educators and clientele
- Identification of clear pathways for applying evaluation findings

These attributes are consistent with key factors identified by Sandison (2006) as facilitating evaluation use: creative and adaptive use of evaluation methods attuned to specific contexts, clear focus on evaluation use and users, the critical importance of trust and relationship between evaluators and evaluation users, appropriate involvement of stakeholders, and clear emphasis on application of evaluation-based learning for improved program performance.

Conclusion

The vantage points explored in this chapter—published Extension evaluation studies and studies identified as exemplary by Extension evaluation professionals—combine to portray a span of evaluation practice ranging from modest program feedback to comprehensive organizational assessments. Do evaluation studies have strong, constructive influences on the Cooperative Extension System? The studies examined consistently yielded specific and valuable program counsel applicable to Extension education practice. Beyond simply generating a supply of potentially useful findings, there was clear evidence of actual and substantive program modification in response to program evaluation. Readily available examples indicated that evaluation studies had influenced Extension practice by helping to establish program direction, improving existing educational practice, informing public policy, establishing or sustaining program support, offering a basis for resource allocation decisions, influencing relationships with stakeholders, and strengthening evaluation practice itself. Clearly, evaluation practice is both dynamic and influential within the Cooperative Extension System.

References

Aguilar, C., & Thornsbury, S. (2005). Limited resources, growing needs: Lessons learned in a process to facilitate program evaluation. *Journal of Extension, 43*(6). Retrieved December 1, 2007, from http://www.joe.org/joe/2005december/a3.shtml

Betz, D. L., & Hill, L. G. (2006). Real world evaluation. *Journal of Extension, 44*(2). Retrieved December 1, 2007, from http://www.joe.org/joe/2006april/rb9.shtml

Clavijo, K., Fleming, M. L., Hoermann, E. F., Toal, S. A., & Johnson, K. (2005). Evaluation use in nonformal education settings. In E. Norland & C. Somers (Eds.), *Evaluating nonformal education programs and settings. New Directions for Evaluation, 108,* 47–55.

Dollahite, J., & Scott-Pierce, M. (2003). Outcomes of individual vs. group instruction in EFNEP. *Journal of Extension, 41*(2). Retrieved December 1, 2007, from http://www.joe.org/joe/2003april/a4.shtml

Gregory, P., Camarillo, J., Campbell, D., Dasher, S., King, N., Mann, M., et al. (2006). Learning from Latino community efforts. *Journal of Extension, 44*(3). Retrieved December 1, 2007, from http://www.joe.org/joe/2006june/a3.shtml

Jacobs, F. (1988). The five-tiered approach to evaluation: Context and implementation. In H. B. Weiss & F. H. Jacobs (Eds.), *Evaluating family programs* (pp. 37–68). Hawthorne, NY: Aldine de Gruyter.

Journal of Extension. (2007). *Welcome to the Journal of Extension.* Retrieved December 1, 2007, from http://www.joe.org/index.html

NEW DIRECTIONS FOR EVALUATION • DOI: 10.1002/ev

Kelsey, K. D., Schnelle, M., & Bolin, P. (2005). Increasing educational impact: A multi-method model for evaluating Extension workshops. *Journal of Extension, 43*(3). Retrieved December 1, 2007, from http://www.joe.org/joe/2005june/a4.shtml

Mincemoyer, C., & Perkins, D. F. (2005). Measuring the impact of youth development programs: A national on-line youth life skills evaluation system. *Forum for Family and Consumer Issues.* Retrieved December 1, 2007, from http://www.ces.ncsu.edu/depts/fcs/pub/forum.html

Perkins, D. F., & Mincemoyer, C. C. (2007, April). *PA 4-H Youth Development life skills study results.* University Park, PA: Penn State Cooperative Extension. Retrieved December 1, 2007, from http://pa4h.cas.psu.edu/

Sandison, P. (2006). The utilisation of evaluations. In Active Learning Network for Accountability and Performance in Humanitarian Action (Ed.), *Key messages from ALNAP's review of humanitarian action* (pp. 13–19). London. Retrieved December 1, 2007, from http://www.alnap.org/publications/RHA2005/RHA05KMS_English.pdf

Suarez-Balcazar, Y., Hellwig, M., Kouba, J., Redmond, L., Martinez, L., Block, D., et al. (2006). The making of an interdisciplinary partnership: The case of the Chicago Food System Collaborative. *American Journal of Community Psychology, 38,* 113–124.

Suarez-Balcazar, Y., Martinez, L. I., Cox, G., & Jayraj, A. (2006). African Americans' views on access to healthy foods: What a farmers' market provides. *Journal of Extension, 44*(2). Retrieved December 1, 2007, from http://www.joe.org/joe/2006april/a2.shtml

Taylor-Powell, E., & Calvert, M. (2006). *Wisconsin 4-H Youth Development: Arts and Communication Program evaluation.* Retrieved December 1, 2007, from http://www.uwex.edu/ces/pdande/evaluation/pdf/064harts.pdf

Trochim, W. M. (1999). *The research methods knowledge base.* Retrieved December 1, 2007, from http://www.socialresearchmethods.net/

Weerts, D. J. (2005). Validating institutional commitment to outreach at land-grant universities: Listening to the voices of community partners. *Journal of Extension, 43*(5). Retrieved December 1, 2007, from http://www.joe.org/joe/2005october/a3.shtml

MICHAEL W. DUTTWEILER is assistant director for program and professional development, Cornell University Cooperative Extension.

Patton, M. Q. (2008). sup wit eval ext? In M. T. Braverman, M. Engle, M. E. Arnold, &
R. A. Rennekamp (Eds.), *Program evaluation in a complex organizational system: Lessons
from Cooperative Extension. New Directions for Evaluation, 120,* 101–115.

8

sup wit eval ext?

Michael Quinn Patton

Abstract

*Extension and evaluation share some similar challenges, including working with
diverse stakeholders, parallel processes for focusing priorities, meeting common
standards of excellence, and adapting to globalization, new technologies, and
changing times. Evaluations of extension programs have helped clarify how
change occurs, especially the relationship between knowledge change and behavior change, the importance of systems thinking, the purposes of evaluation
(accountability versus improvement versus knowledge generation), the
significance of process use, and the challenge of matching methods to evaluation
questions, resources, and purposes to ensure methodological appropriateness.*
© Wiley Periodicals, Inc.

xtension's mission is *extending* the knowledge of universities to
improve lives and help solve community problems. As Extension
approaches its hundredth anniversary in the United States, its story
is one of continual adaptation and change, including evolving evaluation
criteria for what constitutes success. The title of this article is meant to capture this sense of change. As I was writing this chapter, I e-mailed my adult
children (ages 35, 29, and 26):

NEW DIRECTIONS FOR EVALUATION, no. 120, Winter 2008   © Wiley Periodicals, Inc.
Published online in Wiley InterScience (www.interscience.wiley.com) • DOI: 10.1002/ev.279

Hey, next generation, I need text message help.

I'm writing an article on lessons learned from evaluating Extension programs. To highlight Extension's adapting to changing times, including new technology and a new generation (think 4-H), I'm considering making the title a text message to connote new ways of communicating. Since I don't text much myself, I don't know the shortcuts.

A straight title might be: What's happening in evaluating Extension? How would you text that?

Papa Evaluandus dinosaurus.

I also got entries from the avid-texting teenage son of a colleague and a 59-year-old regular texter. Here are the responses:

sup wit eval ext?

xt, waz happnin

ne 411 on eval ext? ltsgt2gthr l8r.

whts up w ext. eval? txt me ur thots

wuts doin wit eval extends?

Translating knowledge from the academic jargon of the university to the language of ordinary people has been a mainstay of Extension. Questioning whether ordinary people understand Extension messages has been a mainstay of Extension evaluation. So, *sup wit eval ext?*

Global Extension

The contributions in this issue focus on the United States, but both Extension and evaluation are global in scope and impact. My Peace Corps assignment in Burkina Faso in 1967 (then Upper Volta) was in the agricultural extension system created by the French colonial administration. Extension was called *vulgarization,* which translates as popularizing, or more colloquially, "taking to the people." We were *agents de la vulgarization.* Because we were engaged in community development, we were also called *animateurs* (organizers) or, as translated by volunteers, "trying to get some-damn-thing done."

I worked with the Gourma people in rural villages where subsistence farmers grew millet and sorghum. Soils were poor, water scarce, and infant mortality high. Infectious diseases were common and debilitating. Markets were underdeveloped and resources few. We were young, idealistic, and clueless. We began with farmers' stories, listening for their perspectives and needs. Gradually, project possibilities emerged: digging wells, building one-room schools, introducing cash crops, and organizing cooperatives. Our efforts were pragmatic and modest.

My approach to evaluation grew out of those seminal community development experiences in Africa. I learned how to bring people together to identify needs and match initiatives to those needs. I learned to ground change efforts in the perspectives of those with whom I worked, trying to be of use to people struggling to survive in a harsh environment. Later, when I began doing evaluations, it was clear from the beginning that I was not going to be the primary user of findings. My niche would be facilitating use by others. I drew on what I had learned about how to ground my efforts in the needs of those with whom I worked, appreciating these people as the primary stakeholders (Patton, 2004). That was the beginning for me of an important connection between Extension and evaluation.

Connecting Extension and Evaluation

In the 1980s, I directed the Caribbean Agricultural Extension Project, serving 10 countries in the Windward and Leeward islands, plus Belize. That led to an evaluation appointment in the Minnesota Extension Service, during which time I became editor of the *Journal of Extension*, which Michael W. Duttweiler sampled for his study in this issue. In working to introduce evaluation to Extension staff around the world, I often began with an exercise comparing extension and evaluation challenges, trying to help Extension staff and program participants connect with this alien and often fear-inducing notion of *evaluation*. Table 8.1 shows an example. Basically, this exercise established that Extension educators work to get people to use information—*and so do evaluators*. Extension educators spend a lot of time considering how to overcome resistance to change. *So do evaluators*. Extension educators worry about communicating knowledge in a form people can understand and use. *So do evaluators*.

This exercise works with many kinds of programs, not just Extension. I learned in Extension that people were more receptive to evaluation if they understood it from within their own worldview.

Table 8.1. Parallel Extension and Evaluation Processes

Basic Extension Processes	*Basic Evaluation Processes*
Step 1: Determine who is to be served by an Extension program. Who are the clients or targets of a program?	Step 1: Determine whose information needs are to be met by an evaluation. Who are the decision makers and primary intended users for the evaluation?
Step 2: Determine the information and program needs of the clients.	Step 2: Determine the evaluation information needs of the decision makers and primary intended users.
Step 3: Gather the needed information and develop the needed program.	Step 3: Gather the needed information.
Step 4: Deliver information and recommendations to clients.	Step 4: Present evaluation findings to the decision makers and primary intended users.
Step 5: Work with clients to apply and use what they've learned.	Step 5: Work with the decision makers and intended users to apply and use evaluation findings.

Going over the Joint Committee Standards (1994) presented another way to make this connection. The Standards articulate the characteristics of a high-quality evaluation. For each evaluation standard there is a corresponding standard for Extension programming. Table 8.2 presents parallel statements for utility standards of both Extension and evaluation.

Different Criteria for Different Programs

The contributions in this issue identify a variety of approaches to evaluating Extension programs that have implications for evaluating any kind of change effort. In their Chapter One, Franz and Townson present a matrix that distinguishes Extension programs along two dimensions—process and content—yielding four "domains" that differentiate Extension approaches. For evaluation purposes, however, what is important is that the different approaches implicitly point to different criteria of effectiveness. Table 8.3 presents the primary evaluation criterion for each approach. Different stakeholders are involved with these distinct approaches, and one of the ongoing debates within Extension is which of these approaches should have priority. Some Extension units want to get out of the business of supplying services and focus on community change. Others want to make educational content the focus. More on this debate later.

Table 8.2. Utility Standards for Extension and Evaluation

Extension Utility Standards	Evaluation Utility Standards
Ensure that an Extension program will serve the information needs of targeted audiences.	Ensure that an evaluation will serve the information needs of intended users.
Extension Principle	**Evaluation Standard**
1. *Targeting Extension education:* Extension programs should be developed to meet the identified needs of specifically targeted audiences.	1. *Targeting evaluation stakeholder identification:* Persons involved in or affected by the evaluation should be identified, so that their needs can be addressed.
2. *Information clarity:* Extension education materials and information should be clear and understandable, including the research base from which the information has been extracted and translated.	2. *Report clarity:* Evaluation reports should clearly describe the program being evaluated, including the program context and the purposes, procedures, and findings of the evaluation, so that essential information is provided and easily understood.
3. *Extension impact:* Extension programs should be planned and implemented in ways that encourage follow-through by clients and program participants, to increase the likelihood that Extension education will be used.	3. *Evaluation impact:* Evaluations should be planned, conducted, and reported in ways that encourage follow-through by stakeholders, to increase the likelihood that the evaluation will be used.

Table 8.3. Extension Approaches and Evaluation Criteria

Extension Approach	Corresponding Evaluation Criteria
1. Service	1. Client and consumer satisfaction
2. Facilitating groups to agree on action	2. Group consensus and subsequent action
3. Content transmission (educational outreach)	3. Learning outcomes and adoption of new practices
4. Transformative long-term change relationships	4. Systems changes on community indicators, e.g., environmental quality, economic vitality

Table 8.4. Alternative Approaches to Agricultural Extension and Corresponding Measures of Success

1. **The general agricultural extension approach.** Success is measured in terms of the rate of take-up of the recommendations and increases in national production.

2. **The commodity specialized approach.** The measure of success is usually the total production of the particular crop.

3. **The training and visit approach.** Success is measured in terms of production increases of the particular crops covered by the program.

4. **The agricultural extension participatory approach.** Success is measured by the number of farmers actively participating and benefiting, and the continuity of local extension organizations.

5. **The project approach.** Short-run change is the measure of success.

6. **The farming systems development approach.** Success is measured by the extent to which farming people adopt the technologies developed by the program and continue using them over time.

7. **The cost-sharing approach.** Success is measured in terms of farm people's willingness and ability to share some of the cost, either individually or through their local government units.

8. **The educational institution approach.** The measure of success is the farming people's attendance at and participation in the school's agricultural extension activities.

Source. Food and Agriculture Organization (2001).

Alternative emphases become even more diverse when we shift to the global stage. Table 8.4 presents eight approaches assessed by the Food and Agriculture Organization of the United Nations (FAO, 2001) in search of worldwide agricultural and rural extension "options for institutional reform in the developing countries." In this framework, based on George Axinn's (1988) guide to alternative extension approaches, what is especially instructive is that each approach is distinguished by specific success criteria. Thus evaluative thinking is built into the very definitions that differentiate these alternatives.

Debate About Priority Outcomes

Rennekamp and Engle trace the emergence of an outcomes evaluation focus in Extension to diffusion of innovations theory, adult education research, Bennett's results hierarchy, and logic modeling. They document the mounting pressure for accountability that came from the external environment and the growing commitment to effectiveness and learning among highly committed Extension professionals. Logic modeling deserves special attention in this regard.

Ellen Taylor-Powell, coauthor of the chapter on evaluation capacity building, has made a stellar contribution to Extension in particular and evaluation in general, through the work she and colleagues have done in making the logic of logic modeling widely accessible. The University of Wisconsin Web site (see Chapter Five) is the first place I send people looking for technical assistance on logic modeling. I can independently confirm the importance and success of logic model diffusion as described in the Taylor-Powell and Boyd chapter.

Rennekamp and Engle conclude that the lasting impact of outcomes evaluation has been to "entrench behavioral change as a logical and valued outcome of Extension programming." This is a significant development. Two decades ago, the pressure for outcomes evaluation spotlighted a contentious debate about Extension's mission and whether behavioral change was indeed the priority outcome. Within universities, faculty who viewed Extension's educational mission as primary argued that the outcomes for which they should be held accountable stopped with increased knowledge; they did not expect to be held accountable for whether people changed their behaviors and actually adopted new practices. Their job was to give people research findings and knowledge that would allow them to make their own decisions. Staff who took this position called themselves Extension *educators*— emphasis on education.

The opposing perspective was that increased knowledge, or more broadly KASA change (knowledge, attitudes, skills, aspirations), is an interim outcome that should lead to practice change—adopting new behaviors and technologies. With behavior change as the mission, it is not enough to just measure knowledge change through increased scores on pre-and post-instruments. The real test is that increased knowledge leads to behavior change. Those who take this position emphasize that Extension staff are *change agents* and Extension should be accountable for bringing about real change. I am assured by the authors in this issue that this is the view that has largely prevailed.

As King and Cooksy comment, this issue also has measurement implications in that Extension evaluations sometimes "confuse" measures of teaching effectiveness with measures of the degree to which those educated have *adopted* the practice taught. "In other words, because of the difficulty in getting accurate measures of adoption behavior, there is sometimes a tendency to focus on *what* is being taught rather than *how effective* the teaching is in changing the behavior of participants" (Chapter Three).

I want to connect this debate about outcomes accountability and measurement to the earlier review of approaches to and typologies of Extension programming. Embedded in those typologies are contrasting views about Extension's mission.

For over a decade, Dick Krueger and I taught an extension evaluation course at the Minnesota Extension Summer Institute. Every year, this debate between the educators and the change agents flourished. Senior Extension administrators typically emphasized the responsibility to show that Extension was solving societal problems by bringing about change. That, they emphasized, is what state legislators, county commissioners, Congress, and the Office of Management and Budget (OMB) expected. It was against change indicators that Extension would ultimately be held accountable. In contrast, university professors who held appointments as Extension specialists emphasized the difficulties of converting knowledge into practice. Their jobs focused on education. They insisted that they could not, and would not, be responsible and accountable for something over which they had no control (behavior change).

The lines of demarcation did not always correspond with job title. In addition to teaching evaluation to hundreds of professionals, I have consulted over the years with some 20 state Extension systems. I've worked with senior administrators who would publicly advocate a practice change perspective but privately admit sympathy for the more limited educational perspective. And I've worked with a large number of university faculty committed to practice change who conducted evaluations focused on behavioral outcomes. The debate has withered, in part because Extension evaluations over the years have increasingly included and measured behavioral outcomes and rates of adoption of new practices. Outcomes evaluation clarified the issues in the debate and helped Extension leadership coalesce around behavior change as Extension's mission. However, the debate has not completely disappeared.

Over the last three years, I facilitated an organizational development (OD) process for a major land-grant university institute with an outreach mission. The interdisciplinary institute includes Extension specialists as well as other faculty who teach, conduct research, and engage in service (outreach) on issues that are a priority for the institute. The OD process involved revisiting the institute's mission; operationalizing the mission with clear, specific, and measurable outcomes; and aligning promotion and tenure criteria with those outcomes. More than 60 faculty and staff participated. The central issue was whether the mission was education or change. The early consensus was that the institute should commit to measurable impact on specific problems by bringing about adoption of new practices and policies. Then the discussion shifted to how those criteria should be operationalized in faculty promotion and tenure criteria—for example, soliciting assessments about the contributions to change of institute faculty from community people, professionals in collaborating organizations outside the university, and policymakers. In the end, the faculty defeated the proposal to align promotion and tenure criteria with change outcomes. The director, who was committed to a practice change mission, resigned.

In the past, such debates were primarily academic. But outcomes evaluation and the transparency that accompanies public accountability have increased the stakes. The results chain and logic modeling are not just useful conceptual tools for program planning and evaluation. Properly used, they demand priority setting. Prioritizing outcomes goes to the heart of organizational mission. Evaluation insists that accountability priorities be made explicit and taken seriously—and the results measured.

Evaluation's Parallel Challenge

I began with comparisons between Extension principles and evaluation standards. Let's continue in that comparative mode by considering the implications of Extension's outcomes debate for evaluation. The evaluation profession faces the same divide over whether evaluators have responsibility for use. Many in evaluation essentially take the position of Extension educators, that the evaluator's job is to produce high-quality findings and present those findings in an understandable manner—*end of job*. The evaluator is not responsible for and cannot be held accountable for whether and how those findings are actually used. Berk and Rossi (1999) epitomize this view:

> …an evaluation may be successful even if the information provided is ignored, or even misused. Once the findings are presented in a clear and accessible fashion, the evaluation is over. What follows is certainly critical, but it is essentially a political process. Interested evaluators are best off observing the action at some distance, preferably through safety glasses. (p. 6)

In contrast, utilization-focused evaluation (Patton, 2008) advocates that evaluations should be judged on whether they are actually used to inform decisions and facilitate change. In training sessions and reactions to my writings, the most common objection is against this notion that evaluators have accountability for how their findings are used. In Extension terms, they are comfortable being evaluation *educators* but not being accountable for actual use.

How Change Occurs

A great many programs are built on the assumption that new knowledge leads to attitude change, which leads to behavior change. This hypothesized results chain is testable. Carol Weiss (2000) has commented on the pervasiveness of this logic model:

Many programs seem to assume that providing information to program participants will lead to a change in their knowledge, and increased knowledge will lead to positive change in behavior. This theory is the basis for a wide range of programs, including those that aim to reduce the use of drugs, prevent unwanted pregnancies, improve patients' adherence to medical regimens, and so forth. Program people assume that if you tell participants about the evil effects of illegal drugs, the difficult long-term consequences of unwed pregnancies, and the benefits of complying with physician orders, they will become more conscious of consequences, think more carefully before embarking on dangerous courses of action, and eventually behave in more socially acceptable ways. (p. 40)

The theory seems commonsensical. Social scientists—and many program people—know that it is too simplistic. Much research and evaluation has cast doubt on its universal applicability.

When an evaluator encounters a program theory positing that knowledge and attitude change will produce behavior change, it is appropriate to bring to the attention of those involved the substantial evidence that this model doesn't work in the simple, linear, direct cause-and-effect chain usually depicted. Rennekamp and Engle note that some Extension theories of change acknowledge the influence of environmental factors on behavioral change. Change models based on farming systems, family systems, and ecological systems view individuals as influenced by complex relationships and environmental factors. At the 2002 national conference of the American Evaluation Association, president Molly Engle made systems thinking the focus of the meeting, bringing to the attention of the profession the profound implications for evaluation of systems-based theories of change. This is an important direction for both evaluation (Patton, 2008; Williams & Iman, 2006) and Extension, but my sense is that most Extension programs and evaluation logic models are still designed with simple linear linkages that assume a direct causal connection between knowledge and behavior change.

Continuing to draw parallels between Extension and evaluation, it is worth noting that evaluation theorists are taking a systems approach to use. Kirkhart (2000) has posited an "integrated theory" of evaluation's consequences using the concept of "evaluation influence" as a unifying construct. Kirkhart posits three dimensions of evaluation influence: source of influence (evaluation process or results), intention (intended or unintended), and time (immediate, end-of-cycle, long-term). She is especially anxious to capture effects that are "multidirectional, incremental, unintentional, and instrumental" (p. 7). Mark and Henry (2004) have conceptualized a comprehensive theory of evaluation influence focusing on "the underlying mechanisms through which evaluation may have its effects" (p. 37). They differentiated individual, interpersonal, and collective levels of analysis and hypothesized four kinds of mechanisms: "general influence processes, cognitive and affective (or attitudinal) processes, motivational processes, and behavioral processes" (pp. 40–41). Their comprehensive framework identified and organized 50 factors that can affect an evaluation's influence. Thus both evaluation and Extension face the challenge of bringing systems perspectives to bear in their theories of change. Michael Duttweiler's study of the uses of Extension evaluations (Chapter Seven) documents a variety of uses and confirms utilization factors established in the evaluation literature. The next step for such utilization studies is examining patterns of use through a systems lens.

Systems thinking and mapping is also relevant to the King and Cooksy chapter on evaluating multilevel programs. The federal, state, and local partnerships that characterize Extension's funding, program implementation, and evaluation make for a complicated set of stakeholder relationships. As they note, stakeholder interests vary by level, and impact measures considered significant at one level may not be accepted as appropriate evidence by decision makers at another level. Moreover, national initiatives inevitably face issues of implementation fidelity. How closely must implementation of a program at the local level follow an original blueprint? How much can implementation vary from the original ideal and still be considered the same program? These questions point to one of the central tensions in implementation evaluation: adaptation versus fidelity as a premier evaluation criterion of excellence (Patton, 2008).

Although the chapters in this issue focus on relationships among the various levels of Extension, external partnerships complicate further both the stakeholder constellation and the measurement challenges. Increasingly, Extension undertakes programs in partnership with other government agencies, private sector organizations, and not-for-profit programs. One of the examples examined by Duttweiler in Chapter Seven evaluated such a partnership. When I've conducted evaluation training and consulted with Extension programs, common questions have been: "How do we get credit for our piece of the action?" "How do we disentangle our efforts and outcomes from those of others with whom we collaborate?" One way of dealing with the problem is moving from attribution analysis to *contribution analysis* (Patton, 2008). A contribution analysis produces "a contribution story" (Mayne, in press) that presents the evidence of multiple influences on program outcomes. Outcome Mapping (IDRC, 2007) uses the language of contribution rather than attribution in looking at what various collaborating partners contribute to outcomes.

Competing Purposes: Accountability Versus Improvement Versus Knowledge Generation

Several chapters offer insight into that most fundamental of tensions, the competing purposes of evaluation. Officially and rhetorically, accountability, program improvement, and learning are all valued. But these distinct purposes require different data and create contrasting challenges in the relationships among evaluation staff, program or administrative staff, and external stakeholders. Michael Lambur's chapter on the organizational location of evaluation highlights how the very structure of Extension deepens the competition among purposes. With authorization and funding from the federal government, Extension is subject to all the accountability demands and paperwork requirements of the feds, including OMB requirements to engage in PART and GPRA processes (see the King and Cooksy chapter for details). State governments have their own accountability demands, as do counties. So Extension sits at the nexus of an accountability troika, juggling requirements from competing levels of government. At the same time, as personnel in an organization supporting change and staffed by dedicated professionals, Extension staff express a strong commitment to quality and effectiveness. They want to use evaluation for program improvement. Finally, as academics in a university-based organization, Extension specialists, who are typically tenured or tenure-track professors, want (and need) to use evaluation for knowledge generation. Specifically, they can't afford to spend time on studies that don't lead to scholarly publications. Extension evaluators experience these competing demands on a daily basis.

Taylor-Powell and Boyd present these competing purposes as context for evaluation capacity building. They observe that "evaluation as critical inquiry and learning may be subjugated to *doing* evaluation to satisfy funders or promote programs, with consequences for evaluation design and learning" (Chapter Five). Yet in a Wisconsin survey, they found that 70% reported engaging in evaluation for program improvement. Michael Lambur adds, reflecting on his relationship with program staff: "Through my personal experience, I learned it was far more effective to promote evaluation as a tool for improving programs than helping the organization meet demands for accountability. . . . Results of such evaluations can be used first for program improvement, and then for accountability purposes" (Chapter Four). Michael Duttweiler's review of the uses of Extension evaluations reflects this same division; in his sample of *Journal of Extension* articles, 40% reported program improvement use while 35% reported more accountability-oriented evidence of effectiveness use.

On the surface, these are just different evaluations serving different purposes. Examined more closely, deep and enduring fissures around evaluation purpose are revealed in the contributions in this issue (and in my own experience). The tensions that accompany competing purposes can induce a kind of *organizational schizophrenia*. Schizophrenia is characterized by impairment in the perception or expression of reality manifest in hallucinations, paranoid or bizarre delusions, or disorganized speech and thinking leading to serious dysfunction. Is the metaphor apt? Consider: I have sat through scores of evaluation planning meetings involving the various stakeholders that fund Extension, the different functions of staff (administrative, field staff, and faculty specialists), and the various constituencies that Extension serves. The discussion typically asserts the value of each of evaluation's purposes, finesses and downplays the tensions, and affirms the organization's full commitment to each purpose. I still have the speech an Extension director delivered at an annual conference before some 500 people:

> We will not choose between proving and improving. Accountability and learning go hand in glove. We will generate scholarly knowledge that demonstrates accountability and increases our effectiveness. Our evaluations will support all elements of our mission: teaching, research, and service. We will be accountable, evaluate for program improvement, *and* generate knowledge to inform future programming. *And we will integrate these functions in everything they do.* That integration will be the hallmark of how we do business. We will do all three, do them together, and do them well. That is my charge to you today.

Given such a utopian vision and inspiring rhetoric, why do I consider it *organizational schizophrenia*? Because it ignores the reality that these are competing, even conflicting, purposes. They do not necessarily reinforce each other. They often, I would say typically, undercut each other. This vision of evaluation unity and utopia, widely embraced—especially in Extension—is, in my judgment, a delusion.

Or perhaps I am being too harsh and cynical. My assessment may be colored by the fact that the day before this speech I spent two hours with this director explaining why these separate functions needed to be acknowledged as competing goods, that priorities needed to be established and communicated, and that these different functions needed to be staffed, resourced, incentivized, rewarded, and managed separately. He nodded knowingly, thanked me for my wisdom, and told me that I had been enormously useful to him in helping him decide the central theme of his keynote speech on the morrow. I was, of course, pleased to be of use.

All the authors in this issue live and work within this schizophrenic nexus. That they remain as coherent about and committed to evaluation as they are is a testament to their resilience and professionalism. Be kind to them when you meet them at national conferences. Theirs is not an easy job.

More generally, I find that evaluators in all fields tend to soft-pedal the tensions between different purposes. To convince people of evaluation's value, evaluators regularly make the same speech that the Extension director made. We promise to build systems that integrate evaluation's distinct functions. Options are presented like a Chinese restaurant menu: let's order some accountability, program improvement, summative evaluation, monitoring, and knowledge generation . . . and everyone can share. Oh, and while we're at it, let's order some process use.

Process Use

Ellen Taylor-Powell and Heather H. Boyd do an excellent job explicating how evaluation capacity building creates "infrastructures to support evaluation, that is, the organizational processes that embed evaluative inquiry into the organization." Process use refers to the effects on those involved in evaluation that extend beyond use of findings, including impacts on the program and organization (Patton, 2008). A recent issue of *New Directions for Evaluation* focused on process use (Cousins, 2007; Patton, 2007). Logic modeling is a good example. Those involved in logic modeling typically develop a shared and coherent perspective about the program that has an impact well before any evaluation findings are generated. This is process use. Taylor-Powell and Boyd describe evaluation processes breaking down silos within Extension, facilitating collective action, supporting collaborative inquiry, and enhancing group problem solving.

I explained earlier that I asked my children and some colleagues for help in coming up with a text message title for this chapter. The titles they sent constituted data. I engaged in *findings use* when I selected the title. But in the process of generating findings, our family shared some laughs and learned about each other's texting habits and preferences, learnings that are still having an impact on family communications. That is process use.

The lessons offered by Taylor-Powell and Boyd about evaluation capacity building are worth close examination. They reveal further similarities between Extension and evaluation. Their lessons offer insights into how they are managing the competing purposes of evaluation—for example, their advice to "use external demands for results as the lever, not the control. Calls for accountability can motivate an organization and its staff; use this motivation to build the internal demand and intrinsic motivators that will sustain quality evaluation and build evaluative inquiry" (Chapter Five). Can you visualize the tightrope they are walking?

The Heavy Weight of the Gold Standard

In Chapter Six, Marc T. Braverman and Mary E. Arnold take on another balancing act: making decisions about methodological rigor. Here again, Extension's location in both the university and the community, funded by both government and the university, and facing competing evaluation demands comes into play. Judgments about rigor are context-dependent, not absolute. The context for Extension is its university base, and thus the criteria for rigor derive from traditional scholarly disciplines. This is where we find the heavy weight of the supposed methodological "gold standard" bearing down. They note that randomized control group designs are widely considered "the gold standard for evaluating program impact—that is, the strongest, most convincing type of design" (Chapter Six). But, they explain, randomized designs present challenges, "which sometimes make other design options preferable," especially given problems of money, time, and burden on participants.

In my reading (and maybe it's just me), I detect a defensiveness about not doing more randomized controlled trials (RCTs). Reading Chapter Six recalled for me submissions to the *Journal of Extension* when I was editor. Designs of all kinds would be explained with a list of reasons an RCT was not possible. Ironically, defensively explaining why an RCT isn't possible reinforces the notion that RCTs are the gold standard.

Braverman and Arnold present an Extension RCT evaluation of a food and nutrition program that exemplifies "a high level of rigor." They then review an evaluation of an Extension 4-H program using survey methods that illustrate "a more moderate level" of rigor. They conclude that the 4-H study's level of rigor is "fully appropriate for its evaluation purposes." That is the real methodological gold standard: *methodological appropriateness*. (For a full discussion of appropriateness as the methodological gold standard, see Patton, 2008, especially pages 421–460.)

Appropriateness is the standard affirmed by the American Evaluation Association position statement on "scientifically based evaluation methods" (AEA, 2003). It is the standard asserted in the European Evaluation Society statement on "the importance of a methodologically diverse approach to impact evaluation" (EES, 2007). Likewise, the Network of Networks on Impact Evaluation (NONIE) advocates the standard of appropriateness. NONIE was established by international evaluation offices representing more than a hundred United Nations, World Bank, and other development organizations, plus developing country representatives. NONIE subgroup 2 drafted guidance for conducting impact evaluations highlighting this key message:

> Methods, techniques and approaches for impact evaluation should match the specific circumstances of the evaluation—its purpose, the nature of the intervention, the questions, the level of existing knowledge, and the resources available. *Methodological appropriateness should be considered the "gold standard" for impact evaluation.*
>
> *NONIE (2007)*

So I would say to evaluators everywhere: stop apologizing for not using RCTs. Simply explain how and why the methods used are appropriate to the purpose, resources, timeline, and intended use by intended users of the evaluation. Duttweiler's analysis (Chapter Seven) shows a preponderance of mixed methods in Extension evaluations. As Braverman and Arnold note, evaluators must be prepared to delineate why the methodological choices made were the best available; this means taking the lead in "countering inflexible institutional biases toward specific methodologies such as experimental designs." Agreed. Do so without being defensive. If you meet the true gold standard of methodological appropriateness, say so, head held high, eyes straight ahead, back firm.

thts wuts doin wit ext eval. txt me ur thots & ltsgt2gthr l8r.

References

American Evaluation Association. (2003). *Scientifically based evaluation methods.* Retrieved May 11, 2008, from http://www.eval.org/doestatement.htm

Axinn, G. (1988). *Guide on alternative extension approaches.* Rome: Extension, Education and Communication Service (SDRE), FAO.

Berk, R. A., & Rossi, P. H. (1999). *Thinking about program evaluation* (2nd ed.). Thousand Oaks, CA: Sage.

Cousins, J. B. (Ed.). (2007). *Process use in theory, research, and practice. New Directions for Evaluation, 116.*

European Evaluation Society. (2007). *The importance of a methodologically diverse approach to impact evaluation.* Retrieved May 11, 2008, from http://www.europeanevaluation.org/news?newsId=1969406

Food and Agriculture Organization. (2001). *Agricultural and rural extension worldwide: Options for institutional reform in the developing countries.* Rome: Extension, Education and Communication Service (SDRE), FAO. Retrieved May 11, 2008, from http://www.fao.org/docrep/004/y2709e/y2709e05.htm#TopOfPage

International Development Research Centre. (2007). *Outcome mapping.* Ottawa: IDRC. Retrieved May 11, 2008, from http://www.idrc.ca/en/ev-26586-201-1-DO_TOPIC.html

Joint Committee on Standards for Educational Evaluation. (1994). *The Program Evaluation Standards.* Thousand Oaks, CA: Sage. Retrieved May 11, 2008, from http://www.wmich.edu/evalctr/jc/

Kirkhart, K. (2000). Reconceptualizing evaluation use: An integrated theory of influence. In V. J. Caracelli & H. Preskill (Eds.), *The expanding scope of evaluation use. New Directions for Evaluation, 88,* 5–23.

Mark, M., & Henry, G. (2004). The mechanisms and outcomes of evaluation influence. *Evaluation, 10*(1), 35–57.

Mayne, J. (in press). Addressing cause and effect in simple and complex settings through contribution analysis. In R. Schwartz, K. Forss, & M. Marra (Eds.), *Evaluating the complex.* New Brunswick, NJ: Transaction.

Network of Networks on Impact Evaluation. (2007). *Impact evaluation guidance,* working draft, subgroup 2 (SG2). Retrieved May 12, 2008, from http://www.worldbank.org/ieg/nonie/index.html

Patton, M. Q. (2004). The roots of utilization-focused evaluation. In M. C. Alkin (Ed.), *Evaluation roots: Tracing theorists' views and influences* (pp. 276–292). Thousand Oaks, CA: Sage.

Patton, M. Q. (2007). Process use as a usefulism. In J. B. Cousins (Ed.), *Process use in theory, research, and practice. New Directions for Evaluation, 116,* 99–112.

Patton, M. Q. (2008). *Utilization-focused evaluation* (4th ed.). Thousand Oaks, CA: Sage.

Weiss, C. H. (2000). Which links in which theories shall we evaluate? In P. J. Rogers, T. A. Hacsi, A. Petrosino, & T. A. Huebner (Eds.), *Program theory in evaluation: Challenges and opportunities. New Directions for Evaluation, 87,* 35–45.

Williams, B., & Iman, I. (2006). *Systems concepts in evaluation: An expert anthology* (AEA Monograph). Point Reyes, CA: EdgePress.

MICHAEL QUINN PATTON, *an independent consultant, is a former president of the American Evaluation Association and author of a new, fourth edition of* Utilization-Focused Evaluation.

INDEX

ORDER FORM SUBSCRIPTION AND SINGLE ISSUES

DISCOUNTED BACK ISSUES:

Use this form to receive 20% off all back issues of *New Directions for Evaluation*.
All single issues priced at **$23.20** (normally $29.00)

TITLE   ISSUE NO.   ISBN

_____   _____   _____
_____   _____   _____
_____   _____   _____

Call 888-378-2537 or see mailing instructions below. When calling, mention the promotional code JB9ND to receive your discount. For a complete list of issues, please visit www.josseybass.com/go/ev

SUBSCRIPTIONS: (1 YEAR, 4 ISSUES)

☐ New Order   ☐ Renewal

U.S.   ☐ Individual: $85   ☐ Institutional: $235
CANADA/MEXICO   ☐ Individual: $85   ☐ Institutional: $275
ALL OTHERS   ☐ Individual: $109   ☐ Institutional: $309

Call 888-378-2537 or see mailing and pricing instructions below.
Online subscriptions are available at www.interscience.wiley.com

ORDER TOTALS:

Issue / Subscription Amount: $ _____

Shipping Amount: $ _____
(for single issues only – subscription prices include shipping)

Total Amount: $ _____

SHIPPING CHARGES:

First Item $5.00
Each Add'l Item $3.00

(No sales tax for U.S. subscriptions. Canadian residents, add GST for subscription orders. Individual rate subscriptions must be paid by personal check or credit card. Individual rate subscriptions may not be resold as library copies.)

BILLING & SHIPPING INFORMATION:

☐ **PAYMENT ENCLOSED:** *(U.S. check or money order only. All payments must be in U.S. dollars.)*

☐ **CREDIT CARD:** ☐VISA ☐MC ☐AMEX

Card number _____Exp. Date_____

Card Holder Name_____Card Issue #_____

Signature _____Day Phone_____

☐ **BILL ME:** *(U.S. institutional orders only. Purchase order required.)*

Purchase order # _____
Federal Tax ID 13559302 • GST 89102-8052

Name_____

Address_____

Phone_____ E-mail_____

Copy or detach page and send to: **John Wiley & Sons, PTSC, 5th Floor**
989 Market Street, San Francisco, CA 94103-1741

Order Form can also be faxed to: **888-481-2665**

PROMO JB9ND